IMAGES
of America

OAK LANE, OLNEY, AND LOGAN

D1452054

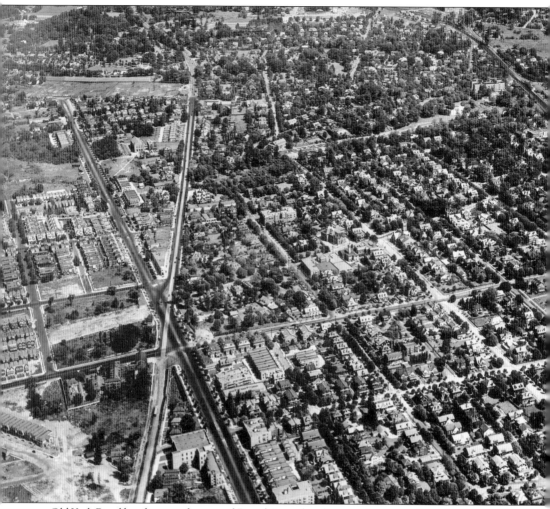

Old York Road heading northeast and Broad Street heading north cross paths to form an intersection. To the right, much of residential East Oak Lane has been developed with large single homes. To the left, tracts of row housing begin to carve into open fields and define West Oak Lane as a more densely populated urban neighborhood. East Oak Lane was developed at the same time as its suburban neighbor to the north, Melrose Park. Both sides of Cheltenham Avenue were called Oak Lane. (Free Library of Philadelphia.)

ON THE COVER: Assorted staff members and hotel guests pose outside the front entrance to the Branchtown Hotel, previously known as the Drover Hotel. Built around 1790, the hotel was located on Old York Road near Church Lane. This historic inn acted as a stopping off point for drovers who brought wagons to market, as well as stagecoach drivers and their passengers. The Branchtown Hotel existed well into the 20th century. (Old York Road Historical Society.)

IMAGES
of America

OAK LANE, OLNEY, AND LOGAN

Marita Krivda Poxon,
Rachel Hildebrandt, and the
Old York Road Historical Society

ARCADIA
PUBLISHING

ISBN 978-0-7385-7386-1

Published by Arcadia Publishing
Charleston, South Carolina

Printed in the United States of America

Library of Congress Control Number: 2010928422

For all general information, please contact Arcadia Publishing:
Telephone 843-853-2070
Fax 843-853-0044
E-mail sales@arcadiapublishing.com
For customer service and orders:
Toll-Free 1-888-313-2665

Visit us on the Internet at www.arcadiapublishing.com

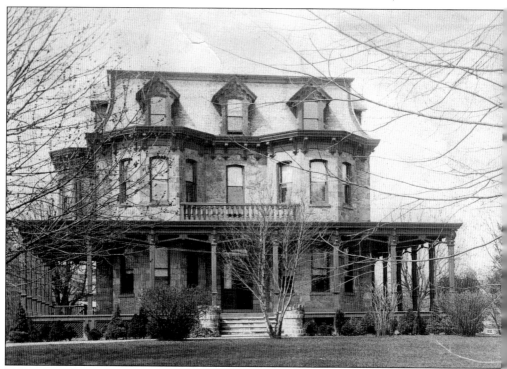

T. Henry Asbury, the father of Oak Lane, initially lived on the north side of City Line (now
Cheltenham Avenue) on an estate named Mestha. He created Asbury Lake by damming the
Saw Mill Creek that flowed through his 115-acre estate, which extended across both sides of
City Line. In 1895, he turned over his residence to a newly formed private school, Miss Marshall's
School for Girls. The school closed in the 1920s, and the mansion was demolished shortly
thereafter. (Germantown Historical Society.)

CONTENTS

PREFACE

In the autumn of 2009, Marita Krivda Poxon organized a series of lectures on the architectural history of East Oak Lane to benefit the Oak Lane Branch of the Free Library of Philadelphia. She utilized the resources of the Old York Road Historical Society, and the deeper she dug, the more interested she became in presenting her research in the form of a publication. Meanwhile, Rachel Hildebrandt, the primary author of our book on architect Horace Trumbauer's buildings in the Philadelphia area, was considering doing a publication on Olney. I was able to bring the two authors together to collaborate on this work, which details the northernmost communities along and adjacent to the Old York Road in Philadelphia. It has been a pleasure to work with both writers, as they brought their wide range of talents to bear in a most rewarding way.

The Old York Road Historical Society formed in 1936 to study and perpetuate the history and folklore of the communities of the Old York Road vicinity, from Rising Sun in Philadelphia to New Hope in Bucks County. While the society is primarily focused on the eight municipalities in the easternmost section of Montgomery County, we still maintain wonderful photographic collections and historical materials that extend all the way down Old York Road in Philadelphia. For these areas, as well as our core communities in Montgomery County, the society continues to collect historical materials. Donations of photographs, manuscripts, and other documents and objects are both strongly encouraged and heartily appreciated. You can discover more about our organization by visiting us on the Web at www.oyrhs.org.

Finally, many thanks to those who support our work through the purchase of this book. We hope that it will not only spark a renewed interest in understanding the history of these remarkably rich communities, but will aid the continuing quest to preserve the best of the past for future generations.

—David B. Rowland, president
Old York Road Historical Society

Acknowledgments

This book would not be possible without the help of many Philadelphia area institutions who both lent images and provided valuable assistance: Bruce Laverty, Michael Seneca, and Susan Gallo of the Atheneaum of Philadelphia (ATH); Laura Beardsley, Alex Bartlett, Judith Callard, Irvin Miller, and Sam Whyte of the Germantown Historical Society (GHS); Karen Lightner, Ted Cavanagh, and Richard Boardman of the Free Library of Philadelphia (FLP); Brenda Galloway-Wright, Anne Mosher, and John Petit of the Temple University Urban Archives (TUUA); William Whitaker and Nancy Thorne of the University of Pennsylvania's Architectural Archives (UPAA); Deborah Boyer of PhillyHistory; Dana Lamparello of the Historical Society of Pennsylvania (HSP); Nicole Joniec of the Library Company of Philadelphia (LCP); Eileen Mathias of the Academy of Natural Sciences; Faith Charlton of the Philadelphia Archdiocesan Historical Research Center (PAHRC); the Reverend Charles Leonard, John Peterson, and Noah D. Hepler of the Lutheran Theological Seminary Archives (LTS); Glenn Colliver of the Episcopal Church Archives (ECA); the Reverend Alonzo Johnson of the Oak Lane Presbyterian Church (OLPC); Robert Hite and Thomas L. McGill of the Episcopal House of Prayer; the Sisters of the Discalced Carmelite Order (DCO); James Butler of La Salle University; Peggy Shelly, Marion Weber, and Dr. Gilda Crozier of Salus University; Gay Johnson, Karen Anderson, and Mark R. Sellers of Awbury Arboretum Archives (AAA); Jean Mansdoerfer Pleis of the *Olney Times*; David Weston of the Oak Lane Community Action Association; Jane Danihel of the Odd Fellows; Barbara Bishop of the North Fifth Street Revitalization Project; Bob Richards of Circus World (Baraboo, WI); Historic American Buildings Survey (HABS); and Naja Killebrew of the Ogontz Avenue Revitalization Corporation.

In addition, many individuals stepped forward with invaluable insights, aid, and images, including the late Elizabeth Adams, Judith and David Chomsky, Dennis DeBrandt, John J. DiBenedetto, Larry Eastwood, Bryan Havir, Andrew Mark Herman, Stevens Hewitt, George Kelly, Janet and Lew Klein, Kirk Lippincott, Craig Mann, Daniel J. McCormick, Janet McShain, Earlene Mitchell, Jefferson Moak, Baron Rowland, Richard C. Ryder, Robert Morris Skaler, Elizabeth B. Smith, David S. Traub, Kelly McShain Tyree, and the Photoworkshop team of Rachel Kotkoskie, Nicki Toizer, and Mike Zaikowski.

We would like to thank our families: T. Michael Poxon, who was a worthy research assistant, coach, and supporter, and Zelda Hildebrandt, who provided assistance and support throughout. The Old York Road Historical Society partnered with us to make this book a reality. The society's invaluable collection of historic materials related to the Old York Road formed the inspiration for and backbone of this book. In addition, we are indebted to the society's president, David B. Rowland, for his mentorship, hardwork, and guidance throughout the entire process of making this book a reality.

Unless otherwise noted, images are from the collection of the Old York Road Historical Society or its sources.

—Marita Krivda Poxon and Rachel A. Hildebrandt

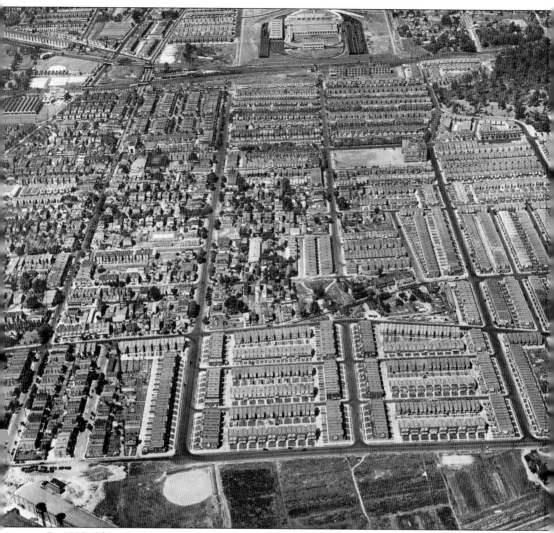

By 1929, Olney had been transformed from rural hinterland into a vibrant urban neighborhood. Its commercial center was at Fifth Street and Olney Avenue, which is visible towards the upper left of this view. (Olney Avenue runs west from lower left.) Stores of every kind, restaurants, theaters, and banks lined Fifth Street, north and south of Olney Avenue. Also visible are Fern Rock Transportation Center (top center) and Fisher Park (top right). The neighborhood's main housing type is the row house. Brand new brick rows were erected by developers beginning in the late 19th century but mostly during the first decades of the 20th century. (FLP.)

INTRODUCTION

The present-day neighborhoods of East Oak Lane, West Oak Lane, Olney, Fern Rock, and Logan share a connected history. They comprise an area that was originally known as Bristol Township in Philadelphia County. The township was bounded north to south by Cheltenham Avenue and the Wingohocking Creek and east to west by the Tacony Creek and Germantown Borough. The first European settler, Quaker Samuel Carpenter, acquired land from William Penn in 1683. He and other settlers transformed the wooded landscape into farmland with small villages at major intersections. The Philadelphia region was often described as "the best poor man's country in the world" because the land was fertile and the climate moderate. Farmers grew a wide variety of produce, and they exported their goods to the city.

As the 18th century progressed, mills producing manufactured goods developed along the Tacony and Wingohocking Creeks. Some of the major mills were located in Grubbtown, Whitaker Mills, Wakefield Mills, and Rowland's Mills. The early roads, such as the Old York Road, the Kensington-Oxford Turnpike (now Rising Sun Avenue), and Olney Road (now Tabor Road) connected Bristol Township to neighboring areas. Villages formed where the roads intersected. Old village names included Branchtown, Milestown, Grubbtown, Wentzville, and Pittville.

On February 2, 1854, Pennsylvania enacted the Consolidation Act of 1854, which incorporated Philadelphia County's 13 townships, 9 districts, and 6 boroughs into the city. Prior to the Consolidation Act, the majority of Philadelphia County's citizens lived beyond the city's borders, which were Vine and South Streets and the Schuylkill and Delaware Rivers. The Consolidation Act abolished the governing structures of the municipalities and consolidated government into a single entity, the City and County of Philadelphia. In addition, consolidation resulted in increased tax revenue, the reorganization of the Philadelphia police department, and the creation of the board of surveyors that created a comprehensive city plan. Essentially, the city plan extended William Penn's grid to the county borders. As development occurred throughout the county during the remainder of the century and well into the 20th century, the City rolled out the grid, demolishing obstacles and paving new streets. Many historic sites were lost, most significantly Solitude in Logan (1903), Champlost in Olney (1909), and Butler Place in West Oak Lane (1925). Simultaneously, several creeks and watercourses, like Logan's Wingohocking Creek, Olney's Rock Run Creek, and East Oak Lane's Saw Mill Creek, were forced underground into sewers to make way for development.

The advent of steam transportation and later electric- and gasoline-powered transportation hastened residential development, and industry and institutions followed. The railroads, the Philadelphia Traction Company's trolleys, the arterial roads (especially Old York Road and Broad Street), and eventually the Broad Street Subway made Oak Lane, Olney, Fern Rock, and Logan accessible and attractive to developers and families. Until this time, the villages of the former Bristol Township shared the common characteristics of large homesteads, farms, mills, schools, and churches. However, as development progressed, the neighborhoods were crafted by developers and the distinctive characteristics of today's communities took root. In East Oak Lane, homebuilders erected mostly large, elaborate detached houses. In contrast, in Olney, Fern Rock, Logan, and West Oak Lane, developers erected mostly row houses. Affordable row houses made the American dream of home ownership possible for many Philadelphians.

In the decades following World War II, Oak Lane, Olney, Logan, and Fern Rock experienced a decline related to the loss of industry and the subsequent population migration to the suburbs. To varying degrees, each neighborhood was confronted with the challenges and issues that many urban areas in the Northeast have faced.

Today there are efforts throughout the area to energize the neighborhoods and business districts through community associations that aim to build upon each area's unique history and character. East Oak Lane is characterized by large, elaborate houses of various styles and grand churches. West Oak Lane boasts houses of practically every size and style, several commercial corridors, and the annual West Oak Lane Jazz Festival. Olney and Fern Rock are distinguished by their history of community spirit and cultural diversity. Logan is the home of notable institutions and schools.

Oak Lane, Olney, Fern Rock, and Logan share a common past as Bristol Township. And, despite the changes that have taken place, each of these neighborhoods is teeming with history. The story of their evolution and development into diverse and vibrant communities is consonant with the stories of Philadelphia's many neighborhoods.

—Marita Krivda Poxon and Rachel A. Hildebrandt

One

EAST OAK LANE

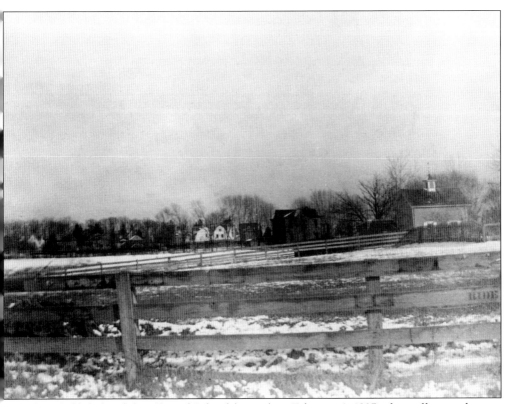

Seen from fields behind the Ellwood School (center) on February 1, 1897, a line of houses denotes Oak Lane. The original name for the Oak Lane area was Milestown, named after Griffith Miles, a Welshman who bought 250 acres of land in 1695. Miles erected a log home along a dirt road that would later be known as Oak Lane, named by Hall W. Mercer as a memorial to an ancient oak tree on his property that blew down during a storm.

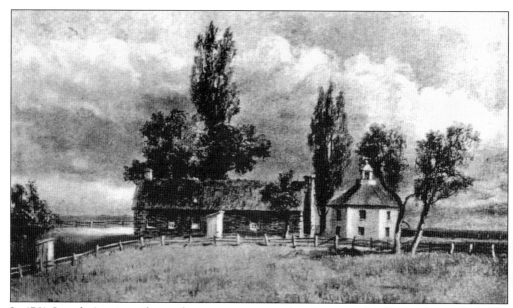

In 1761, Joseph Armitage donated a one-story stone schoolhouse on land located near the Miles house on Oak Lane. Armitage appointed neighbors as the school's first trustees, and parents paid tuition and maintained the building. Originally called the Armitage School and later the Milestown School, the building was used for education and worship services. Alexander Wilson and John Bachman, both American ornithologists, were teachers. (GHS.)

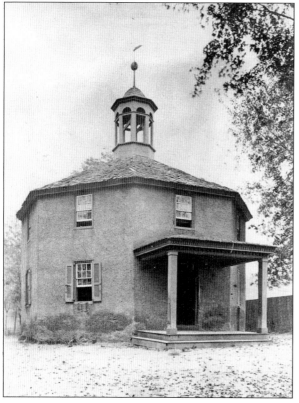

Because of the success of the Milestown School, an adjoining octagonal schoolhouse was built in 1818. It was two stories high, with the second story reserved for church services. Many of the teachers boarded in homes nearby. Students of both sexes and all ages studied subjects like botany, Latin, French, and German. In 1822, two unsuccessful attempts to burn down the school occurred because of a proposed tuition increase. (GHS.)

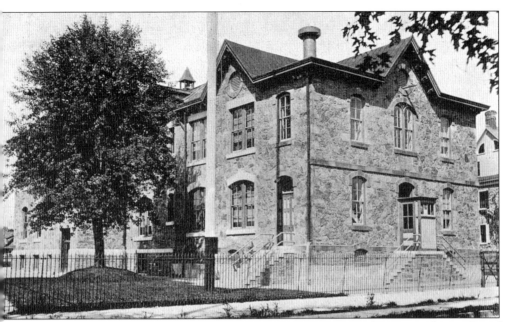

With the development of the Oak Lane area in the latter half of the 19th century, the number of students eventually outstripped the capacity of the Milestown School. The trustees of the school conveyed their property to the Philadelphia Board of Education, which built a public school. Ellwood Elementary School was designed by architect Lewis H. Esler (*fl.* 1843–1883) in 1875. In 1904, architect J. Horace Cook (*fl.* 1887–1931) designed a rear addition.

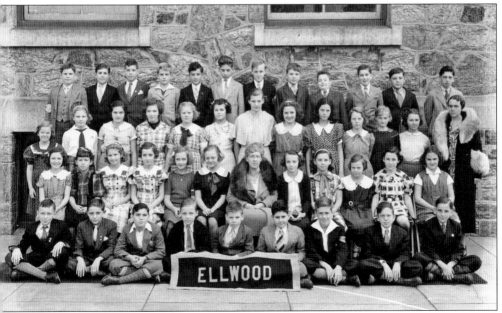

As early as 1924, Oak Lane residents protested because only 350 children out of more than 1,000 could be accommodated in the Ellwood School. Because there were so many students, two classes graduated per year, one in January and another in June. In this photograph, the January 1936 graduating class gathers around school principal Emily Patterson. In 1957, the school was demolished and replaced with a modern building that still stands.

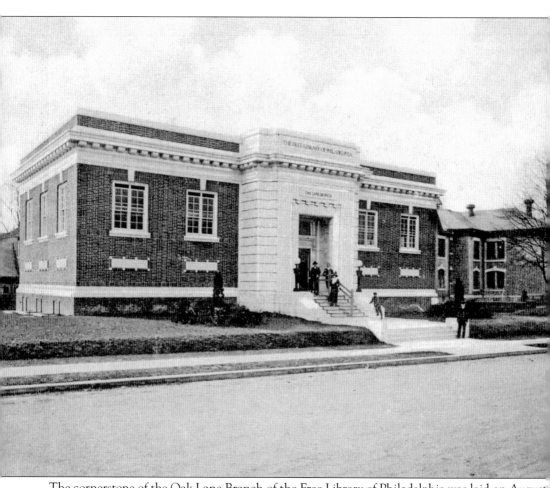

The cornerstone of the Oak Lane Branch of the Free Library of Philadelphia was laid on August 10, 1910, and the building opened to the public on December 7, 1911. The library was designed in the classical revival style by architect Ralph E. White (1886–1948). Andrew Carnegie donated $50,000 to build the library on the condition that the City of Philadelphia provide the site. Oak Lane residents purchased the property at the corner of Twelfth Street and Oak Lane for $5,000 through subscriptions to the library site fund and gave the land to the City. The library served the early community as a gathering place for groups like the Old York Road Improvement League and the Oak Lane Review Club. Today the library continues to serve the needs of the Oak Lane community. (HSP.)

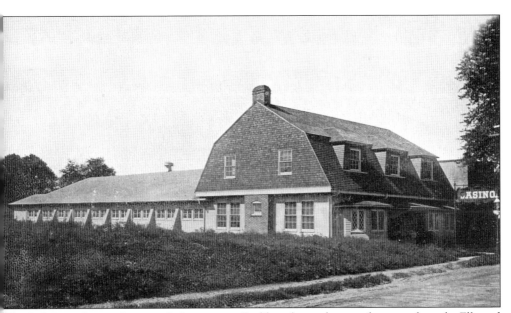

The Oak Lane Casino Company's Amusement Building, located across the street from the Ellwood School, was built in 1887 as a hall for social gatherings. It featured bowling alleys, pool tables, and card tables. The facility operated until 1916 when the company closed. The city acquired the site and converted the building into a firehouse. Up until then, the nearest fire protection was in Branchtown. In 1950, the building was demolished for a new firehouse.

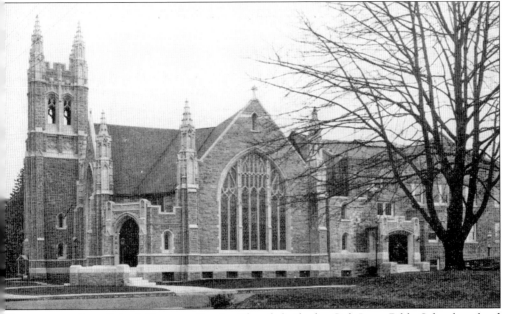

The congregation of the Milestown Baptist Church built the Oak Lane Bible School on land purchased May 14, 1909, at Twelfth Street and Oak Lane. The Bible school was dedicated in December 1914, and a new sanctuary followed in 1922. The Beaux-Arts revival-style church was designed by Philadelphia architect George Savage (1874–1948). In 1972, the Oak Lane Baptist congregation sold their building to St. Mary Protectress Ukrainian Orthodox Church, and in 1984, they folded.

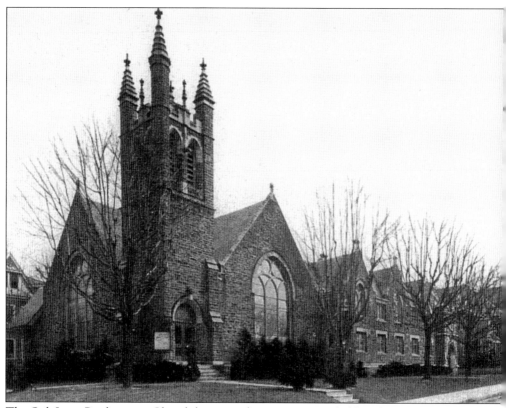

The Oak Lane Presbyterian Church began with prayer services held at the Lawnton Mansion, a summer retreat hotel, in 1891. The congregation built its first church at the southeast corner of Seventh Street and Sixty-sixth Avenue in 1892. Under the leadership of Rev. Oswell G. McDowell, the membership grew to more than 200 families. Ground was broken for a new sanctuary on October 6, 1902, at the southeast corner of Eleventh Street and Oak Lane. Charles W. Bolton (1855–1942) was the architect. (OLPC.)

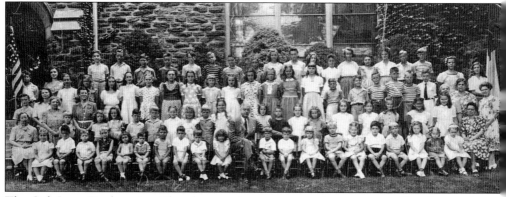

The Oak Lane Presbyterian Church was a large congregation, as attested by the number of children attending daily Vacation Bible School in 1943. However, the church experienced declining membership in the late 1950s. The Reverend Richard S. Armstrong, pastor at the time, organized Operation Bootstrap, which started a neighborhood-wide evangelical outreach campaign. Armstrong would go on to write a book about his "visitation evangelism" called *The Oak Lane Story* (1971). (Dennis DeBrandt.)

The Queen Anne-style Victorian home at 1119 Oak Lane was built around 1898 for Frank Miller. Miller purchased the land from the Joseph Kulp estate, the land having been part of a fruit tree orchard. In 1904, Leo Niessen, a successful Center City florist, purchased the home. Influential architectural pattern books such as A. J. Downing's *The Architecture of Country Houses* (1859) inspired the exodus to the country and fueled dreams to build country "cottages." (TUUA.)

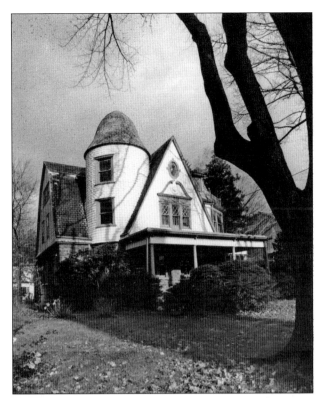

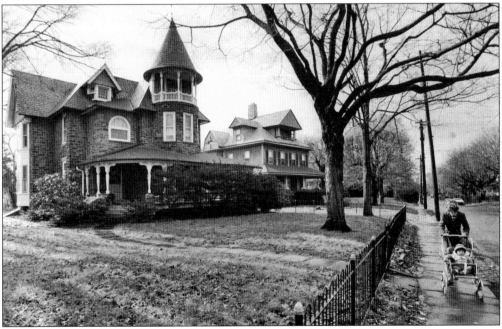

One of America's first female architects, Minerva Parker Nichols (1863–1949), designed the home at 1014 Oak Lane in 1890 for Wallace F. Mum, a wealthy attorney. The house was designed in a high Queen Anne style. Parker built residential housing as well as lectured on historic architectural ornamentation at the Women's School of Design, now the Moore College of Art. (TUUA.)

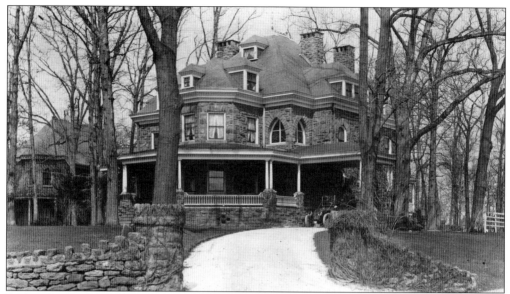

Built in 1855, Northwood (partially visible to the left) was the estate of Theodore M. Delany. The estate fronted onto Lawnton Avenue. Around 1900, Newton Jackson purchased a plot on the Delany property and built his own mansion. The Jackson house showcased an enormous wraparound porch with a porte cochere. The mansion was demolished after a fire in 1939, and Northwood fell to a wrecking ball in 1942. (GHS.)

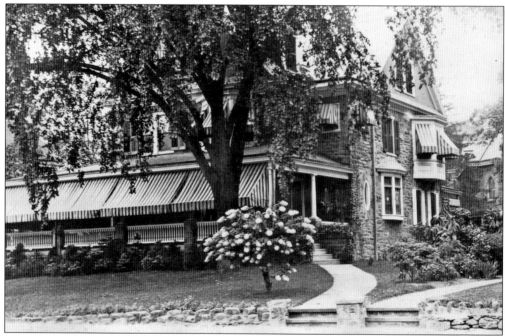

Directly in front of Northwood stands the G. H. Pim home. It was built around 1910 in the Colonial Revival style by noted architect Valentine B. Lee Sr. (*fl.* 1890–1936), who was instrumental in the development of this architectural style in Oak Lane. Local grey stone was used masterfully to create a symmetrical two-and-one-half story residence with a columned front porch and evenly spaced windows. The home still stands. (GHS.)

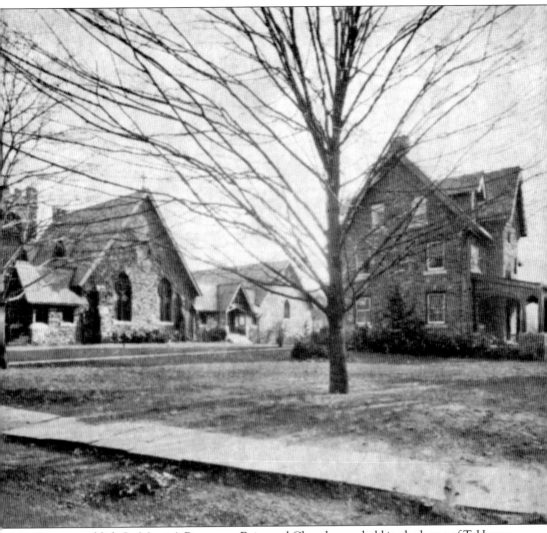

Meetings to establish St. Martin's Protestant Episcopal Church were held in the home of T. Henry Asbury in September 1887. Philadelphia architect Harrison Albright (1866–1932) was chosen to design the church's building. Albright designed this English Gothic Revival church with its own bell tower using local stone with Indiana limestone trim. A two-story parish house designated for classrooms was added onto the church in 1901. In 1904, the architect Isaac Pursell (1853–1910) designed a stone rectory next door to the church. In the early years, the congregation was an active one, attracting many of the socially prominent from the area. However, in more recent decades, declining Episcopalian membership forced the diocese to close the parish and sell the buildings. It is now the Refuge Temple House of Prayer Hebrew Pentecostal. (ECA.)

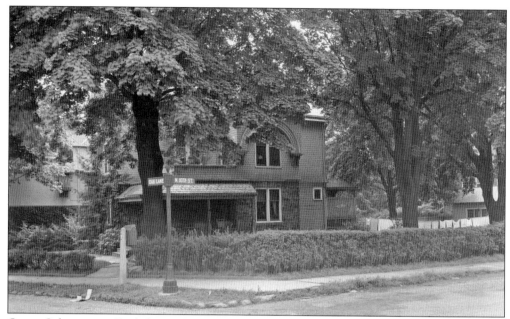

Owen Osborne, an Englishman from a hosiery manufacturing family, came to Philadelphia around 1870 and established his own factory in Kensington. He was awarded numerous patents and trademarks that he used in the manufacture of infant stockings and ladies silk stockings. In 1888, Osborne commissioned the firm of Briean and Godwin (fl. 1886–1889) to build two Queen Anne–style homes, one for his residence at 904 Oak Lane (pictured) and a mirror image at 902 Oak Lane for his daughter Eva May Osborne. In 1902, Osborne's house passed to his son, who in turn sold it to Estelle and Charles Major in 1911. (PhillyHistory.)

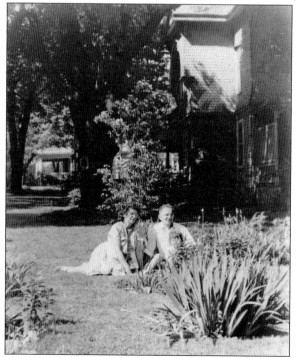

Charles Major's son, Dr. Charles Percy Major, ran an in-home medical practice for 25 years at 904 Oak Lane. He sold his home to Margaret Mary and Adolph Krivda in 1945. In this picture, the new owners sit in the home's garden. Their seven children could roam undeveloped land on either side of Cheltenham Avenue as well as the 6-acre Bromley estate. The children walked eight blocks to Holy Angels Roman Catholic School and participated in the school's sports and music programs. (Marita Krivda.)

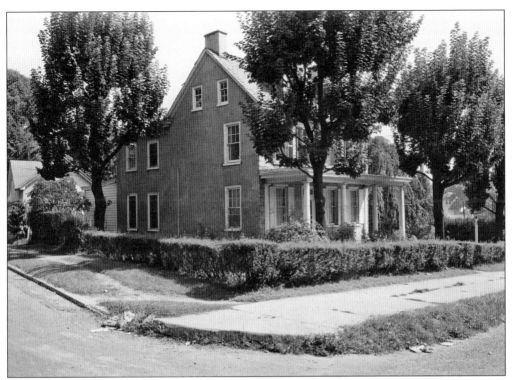

The farmhouse at 821 Oak Lane at Verbena Avenue dates back to the time of the American Revolution. In the mid-1850s, John Grubb, a shoemaker, lived here and he housed two railroad contractors who eventually married his two daughters. These men helped lay the North Pennsylvania Railroad tracks in 1853. During the early 1900s, local physician Dr. Gordon ran a family practice in the home. Another area doctor, Dr. Shinn, later operated out of the home as well. (PhillyHistory.)

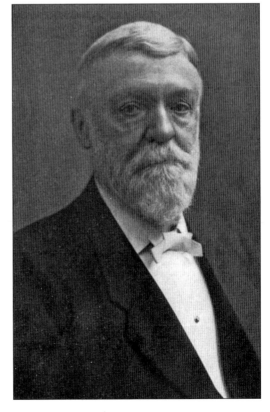

Gen. Louis Wagner (1838–1914) lived at 821 Oak Lane. Born in Germany, his family came to Philadelphia in 1849. At the outbreak of the Civil War, Wagner enlisted and participated in many battles, including the Second Battle of Bull Run and Chancellorsville, where he suffered a permanent disability. He volunteered to command Camp William Penn, which would become the largest federal training facility for African American troops, located in nearby Chelten Hills. After the Civil War, Wagner was involved in many veteran and educational endeavors. (TUUA.)

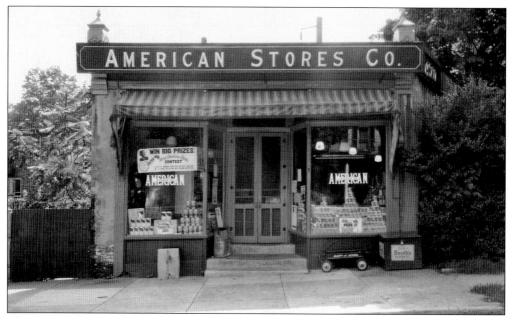

The American Stores Company was a small neighborhood market that stood at 816 Oak Lane in Oak Lane Village since at least 1920. The woodwork and screen door were painted a bright yellow with neighborhood announcements taped to the windows. Small markets like this disappeared with the coming of supermarkets. The Gallelli brothers bought the building where they operated a tailoring and dry cleaning business for 40 years before selling it to the current Korean owners. (PhillyHistory.)

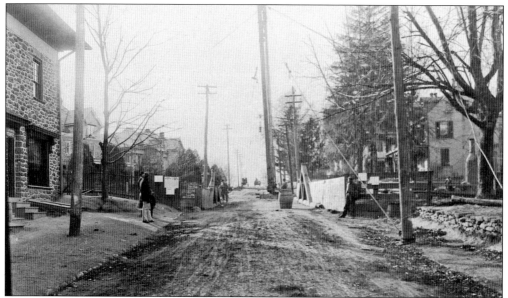

The Oak Lane Bridge crossed over the North Pennsylvania Railroad tracks. In 1876, Thomas S. Lister, who had purchased land from the estate of David Rorer, gifted land for the site of the Oak Lane Station near this bridge at 805 East Sixty-ninth Avenue. The Oak Lane Station was a block north of the bridge on Oak Lane at grade just below City Line. The station was relocated to its current location in Melrose Park in 1905. (PhillyHistory.)

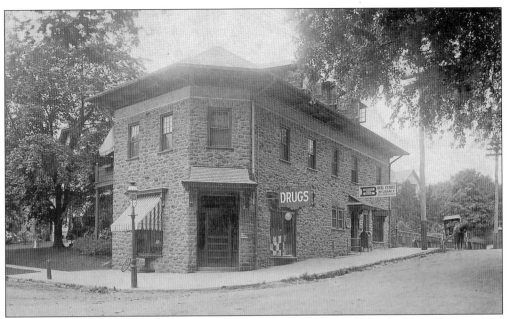

In 1883, a large commercial building was constructed in the heart of the Oak Lane Village. The building housed the post office, a drugstore that was run in its early years by Dr. Klopp, a real estate office, and apartments. For almost 50 years, it was home to John's Meats. The McShain family has owned the building since 1970 and opened Under the Oak Café in 2007. (Andrew M. Herman.)

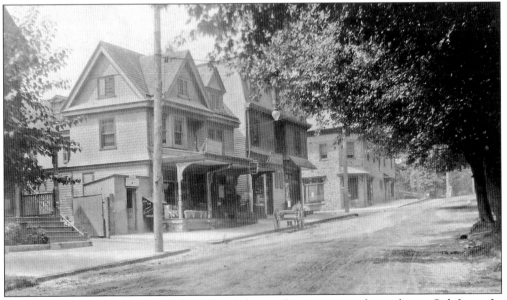

In the early 1900s, Oak Lane Village included several country storefronts facing Oak Lane. In this photograph, the store in the foreground would become Ed's Barber Shop and Mrs. Lane's Beauty Salon. The adjacent corner building was demolished around 1960 for a modern brick structure. The Oak Lane Improvement Association, established in 1917 and a forerunner of the Oak Lane Civic Association, held celebrations for Independence Day along Oak Lane. (Andrew M. Herman.)

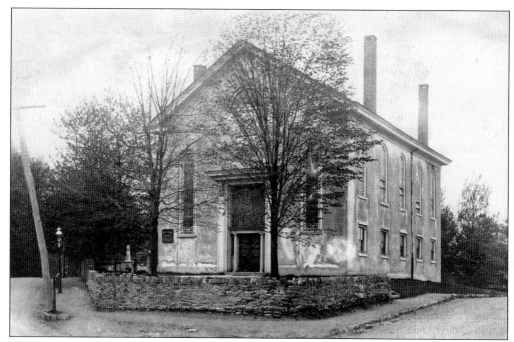

The congregation of the Union Baptist Church of Milestown (later the Oak Lane Baptist Church) had its first meetings in the octagonal schoolhouse. In 1832, David Rorer donated land at the corner of Oak Lane and City Line that soon included a sanctuary, cemetery, and horse sheds. In 1857, a second story was added onto the church with a subsequent remodeling in 1888. The congregation moved to a larger facility in the 1920s and demolished the old church in 1933. (GHS.)

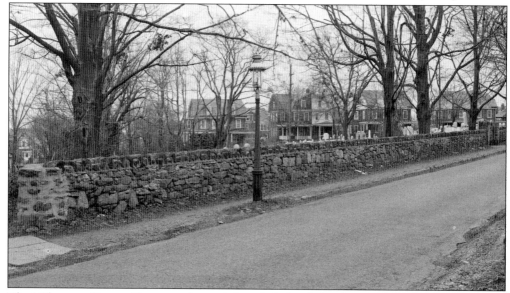

The Milestown Baptist Cemetery, located directly behind the church, contained the graves of area residents interred between 1836 and 1911 and included soldiers who fought in the Civil War. After the Baptist church was demolished in 1933, the cemetery was neglected. The bodies were removed in the 1960s, and the Cheltenham Nursing and Rehabilitation Center now occupies the site. (PhillyHistory.)

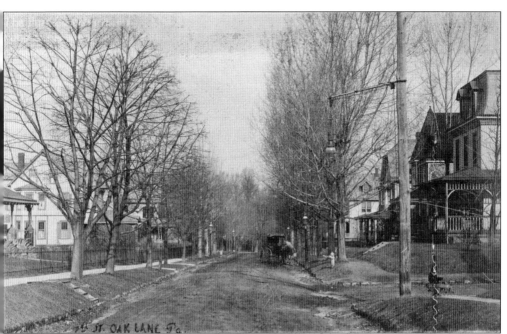

In the late 1890s, the portion of Seventh Street that ran down to Saw Mill Creek was originally called Union Avenue. Kirby's Ditch was where the creek came in at City Line. This view looks north toward Oak Lane with its large, three-story Victorians. Sarah Greenberg lived at 6703 North Seventh Street in the 1920s. She was involved with the National Women's Trade Union League of America. Her sister, Bertha Greenberg, lived nearby at 6801 North Seventh Street.

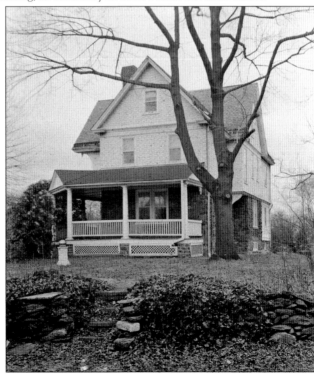

Artist Edward Oswald Wingert (1864–1934), a graduate of the Pennsylvania Academy of the Fine Arts and pupil of Thomas Pollock Anshutz (1851–1912), lived at 506 Oak Lane at the turn of the century. He was a prolific oil painter who often painted rural Oak Lane's buildings, gardens, and people. (PhillyHistory.)

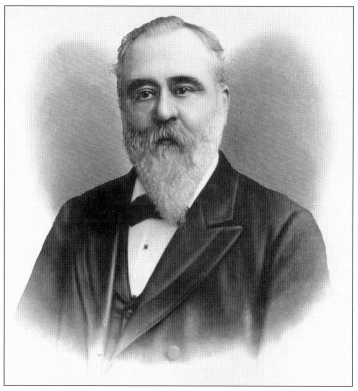

T. Henry Asbury was born on October 19, 1838, in Birmingham, England. He came to America and began work as a machine tool builder. In 1864, Asbury started the Enterprise Manufacturing Company. Its first successful product was a molasses pump. Asbury first purchased land in the area around 1880. He went on to develop the southern portion of his 115-acre holdings and constructed 34 "architectural cottages" along Asbury Terrace and Lakeside Avenue. Asbury died on January 11, 1907, at his winter home in Clearwater Harbor, Florida.

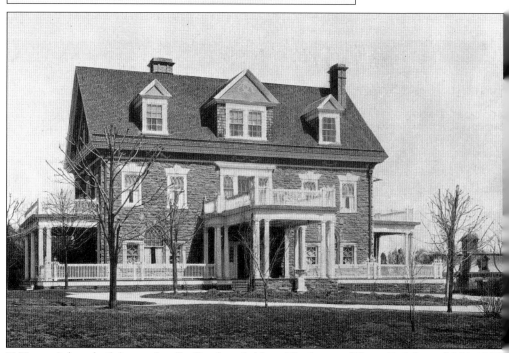

T. Henry Asbury built homes for all of his five children. The home of Harry E. Asbury (1866–1937) still stands at the corner of City Line and Mill Road (now Seventieth Avenue). Architect Amos J. Boyden (1853–1903) designed the three-story, stone Colonial Revival mansion in 1892.

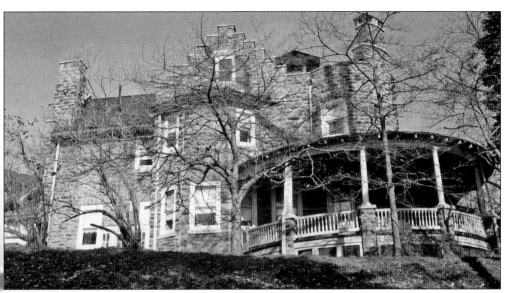

The home given by Asbury to his youngest son, Charles W. Asbury (1870–1935), still stands at 970 West Cheltenham Avenue. This eclectic three-story stone home has a Gothic-style semicircular castle-like tower and a Queen Anne–style asymmetrical wraparound porch. Harrison Albright designed the mansion around 1890 with a commanding view of Asbury Lake and its dramatic weeping willow trees. (John J. DiBenedetto.)

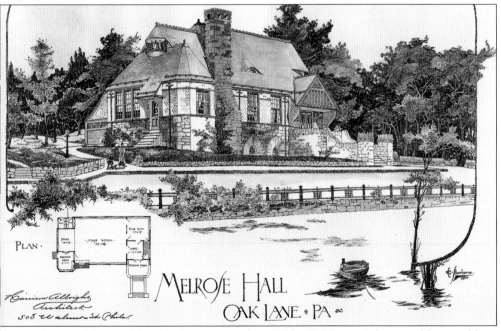

The Melrose Athletic Club of Oak Lane was founded by T. Henry Asbury and his neighbors in December 1887. The following year, the club commissioned architect Harrison Albright to design a suitable clubhouse, named Melrose Hall. Though the club folded in 1894, Asbury retained Melrose Hall. The building was used by many area organizations for dances, theater performances, lectures, receptions, and parties. The building was located on City Line and was demolished in the early 1920s.

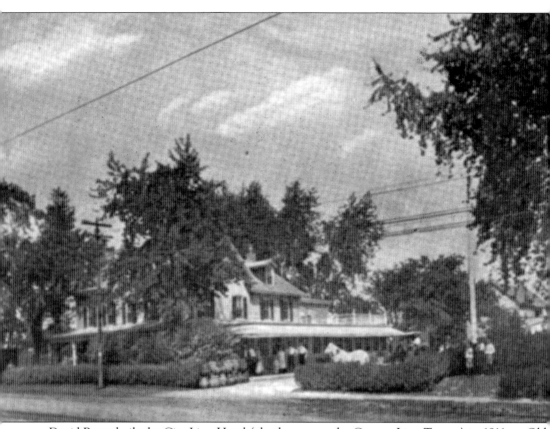

David Rorer built the City Line Hotel (also known as the County Line Tavern) in 1811 on Old York Road at City Line, today's Cheltenham Avenue. Farmers who patronized the hotel brought their produce to Philadelphia on the Tuesdays and Thursdays preceding market days. Beginning in 1833, the Cheltenham and Willow Grove Turnpike Company collected tolls on the Old York Road at a tollgate adjoining the hotel. Around 1892, the hotel lost its liquor license due to the misconduct of the manager and closed. In 1899, the hotel was leased to Thomas F. Curley, who attempted to get the license restored. However, according to a local paper, there was a concern that the hotel would "become a lounging place for the rougher element in the neighborhood, who could violate the law and laugh at the police by crossing the county line." The hotel stood as the City Line Café for many years but was demolished by the mid-1960s when Cheltenham Avenue was widened. The Cheltenham-York Road Nursing Home presently exists on the site. (HSP.)

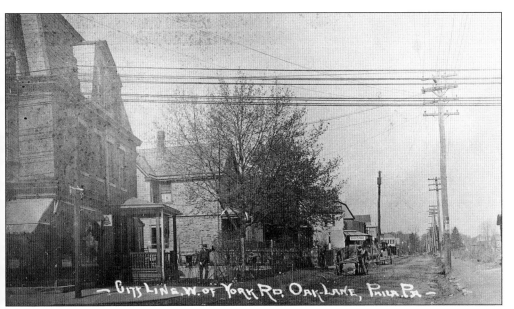

City Line west of Old York Road was not developed until the end of the 19th century. The corner building was constructed in the mid-1880s, while the remaining stores and residences followed at least 10 years later. Prior to development, most of the ground had been owned by Edward M. Davis, the son-in-law of abolitionist and Cheltenham Township resident Lucretia Mott. All the buildings along City Line to Fifteenth Street were removed for the Cheltenham Avenue underpass of Old York Road in the early 1960s.

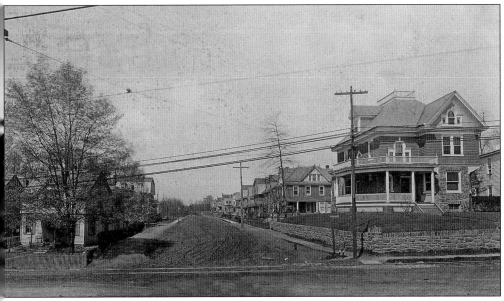

The 1300 block of Seventy-first Avenue between Old York Road and Broad Street was part of the ground developed by the North Broad Street Cottage Lot Association. Broad Street had been opened for several blocks in this area by the association well before it connected either north or south to other sections of the road. The houses on the north side and several on the south side of Seventy-first Street were built around 1900, and virtually all of them still stand. (Andrew M. Herman.)

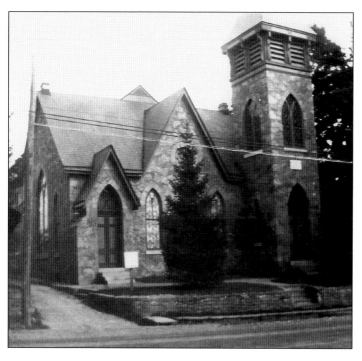

John Wentz, a devout young Methodist and a member of St. James Church in Olney, thought Milestown needed its own church. He secured land and funds, and in 1834 the newly organized congregation built a simple meetinghouse on Old York Road opposite what is now Seventy-first Street. In 1879, the congregation built a new sanctuary in the Gothic style that stood directly in front of the old meetinghouse. The congregation continued to expand, and in 1896 a two-story Sunday school building replaced the old meetinghouse.

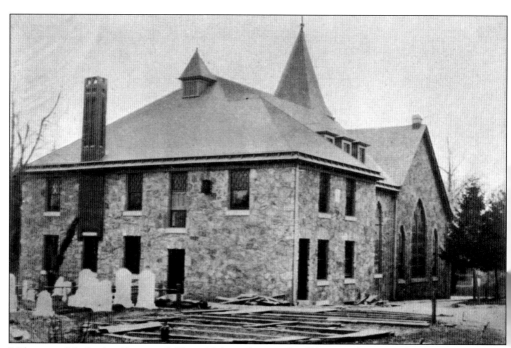

Milestown Methodist Episcopal Church's burial ground still lies on the east side of Old York Road below City Line. Some of the tombstones can be seen behind the 1896 Sunday school addition. The first burial occurred in 1836 and the last in 1934. Tombstone inscriptions bear names linked with the early days of the church and Milestown.

By 1906, when the church's sanctuary was enlarged and remodeled, the congregation was known as the Oak Lane Methodist Episcopal Church. As part of the enlargement, the bell tower was moved to the north side of the building. It was a familiar sight on Old York Road. The tower contained a memorial bell purchased by Susanna Morton in memory of her husband, Samuel Morton. That bell was later moved to the 1924 church tower where it still rings.

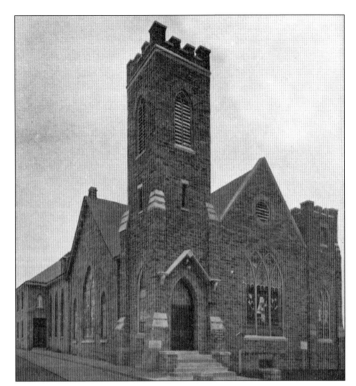

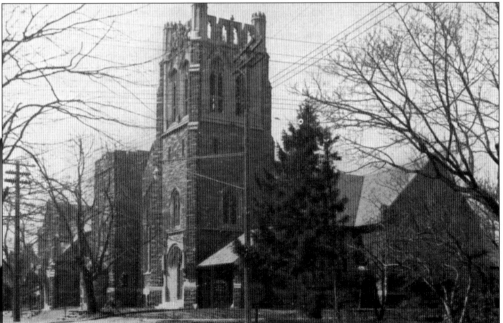

The Reverend John H. Hackenberg purchased property at Twelfth Street and City Line for a new church edifice. Bishop Joseph F. Berry laid the cornerstone on October 18, 1924. Architect Wesley L. Blithe (1873–1946) designed the church in the 15th century Gothic style, which was built for the staggering sum of $345,000. The congregation eventually disbanded in 1981 and sold the church building to the United Korean Church of Philadelphia, which continues to maintain it.

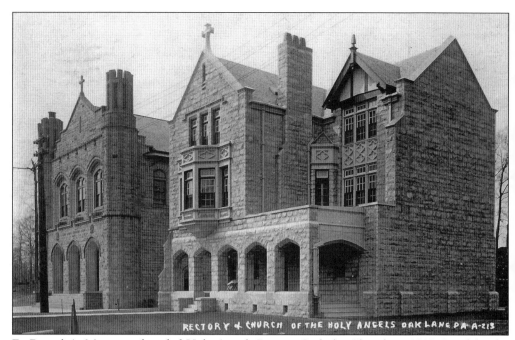

Fr. Daniel A. Morrissey founded Holy Angels Roman Catholic Church in 1900. Land for the new church was purchased along Old York Road at Seventieth Avenue. Archbishop Ryan opened Holy Angels on November 17, 1901. In 1902, a rectory was built. Both buildings were designed by church architect George I. Lovatt Sr. (1872–1958) in the English country Gothic Revival style. In 1905, a school opened on the second floor over the sanctuary. (Andrew M. Herman.)

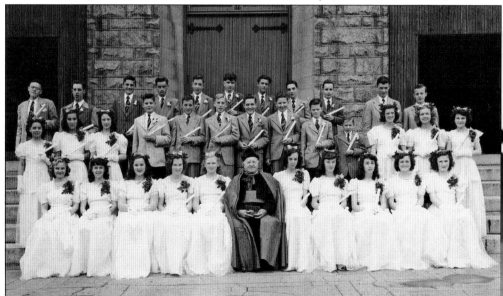

The eighth-grade graduation day photograph from 1947 was taken in front of Holy Angels Church with the Right Reverend Monsignor Bernard A. McKenna (1875–1960). McKenna ran a highly successful parish with a growing parishioner base. In the late 1980s, when demographics were changing in East Oak Lane, the Archdiocese of Philadelphia made Holy Angels the Philadelphia-North Vicariate for Korean Roman Catholics. (Marita Krivda.)

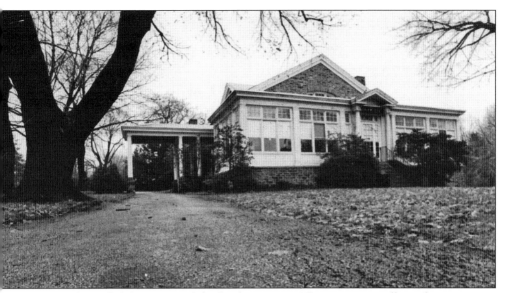

Mary E. Steward founded the Review Club of Oak Lane in 1895 to promote intellectual improvement and to advance the interest of the community. In 1923, club members raised the funds to build a clubhouse at the corner of Seventieth Avenue, Twelfth Street, and Lakeside Avenue. Oak Lane architect William E. Groben (1883–1961) designed the building. Around 1980, the Review Club folded, and the building was sold to a Korean congregation. (TUUA.)

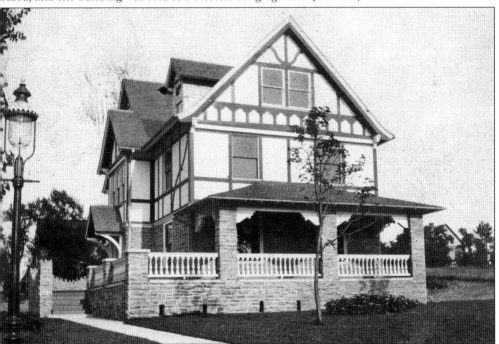

Philadelphia architect Horace W. Castor (1870–1966) designed the Tudor Revival home at 1200 Sixty-ninth Avenue for Edwin S. Radley, a local builder. Dennis B. McGookin, a wealthy inventor, bought the home from Radley. In 1969, a Ukrainian congregation established St. Mary Protectress Orthodox Church and school and occupied the McGookin residence. The church later moved to Twelfth Street and Oak Lane, and the house now sits neglected and unoccupied.

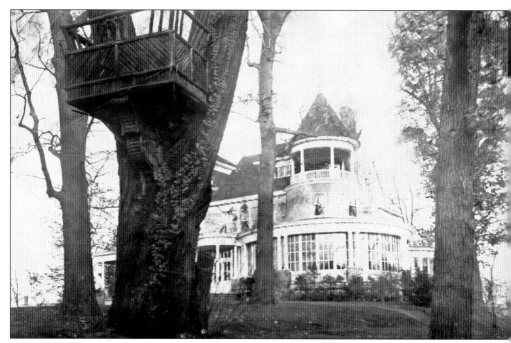

Edward Bromley, a wealthy carpet and textile manufacturer, built his mansion, Lakeside, on 6 acres fronting Old York Road between Sixty-ninth and Lakeside Avenues. He purchased the land from T. Henry Asbury. Bromley, a bachelor, lived there with his two sisters, Phoebe Bromley and Anna Eberbach. After his death, Caroline Kammerer claimed a widow's share of Bromley's $4 million estate. A settlement rumored at $1 million was given to "Mrs. Bromley" by the family. (FLP.)

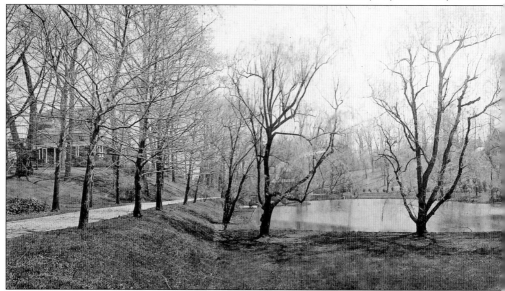

Bromley's Lakeside had its own man-made lake complete with a boathouse, a Japanese foot bridge connected to an observation point, and swans. Hazlehurst and Huckel (fl. 1881–1900), the architectural firm of choice for the Bromley family, likely designed the mansion. Phoebe Bromley lived in the mansion until her death in 1941. The mansion was eventually torn down, and the lake was used for decades by countless children for winter ice skating. (Andrew M. Herman.)

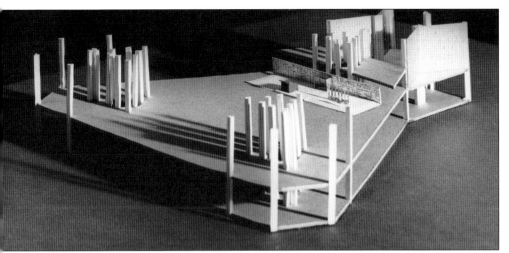

The Congregation of Adath Jeshurun, founded in 1858, purchased Lakeside and considered developing the estate for a new temple following a decision to relocate from their North Philadelphia address. The congregation hired world famous architect Louis I. Kahn (1901–1974) to design a synagogue and school building. Kahn's proposal was dismissed in April 1955 when it failed to win the approval of the entire board. Adath Jeshurun went on to build a new synagogue complex in Elkins Park and put Lakeside up for sale. (UPAA.)

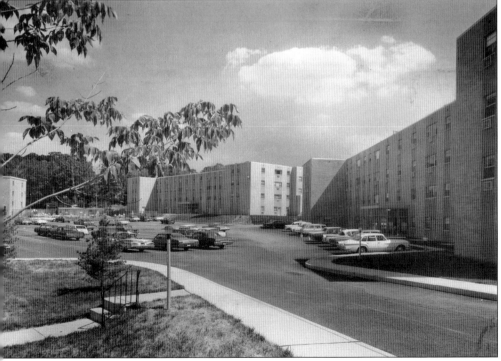

The Oak Lane Civic Association worked to prevent a sale of Lakeside to developers. After several overtures were made to the City to purchase the estate for a park or recreation area failed due to a lack of funds, the Hardy Association, a real estate developer, purchased the property in 1962. Hardy hired architect Armand John Nasuti (b. 1926) to design Bromley House, a three-story, brick, low-rise garden apartment complex that opened in 1966. (TUUA.)

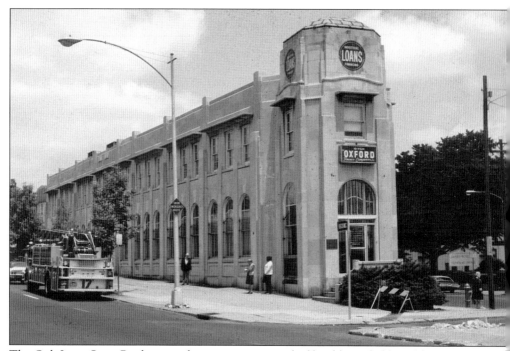

The Oak Lane State Bank secured a prominent parcel of land bounded by Old York Road and Broad Street. To establish itself as a progressive, modern bank for its affluent customers, the bank hired the architectural firm of McLanahan and Bencker (*fl.* 1919–1925) to design an art moderne commercial building in 1922. The long sides of the building with their oversized limestone buttresses created a defined series of bays with a line of arched windows. (John J. DiBenedetto.)

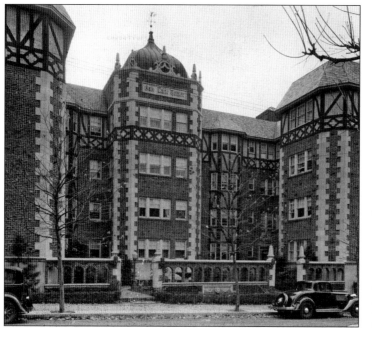

The Oak Lane Arms Construction Company built the Oak Lane Tower Apartments in 1928 at the southeast corner of Thirteenth Street and Sixty-eighth Avenue. Max Bernhardt (1896–c. 1947) designed the building in the Jacobean Revival style with a center tower flanked by two wings. The four-story building contained 52 grand apartments. The building, still standing, has been turned into condominiums. (FLP.)

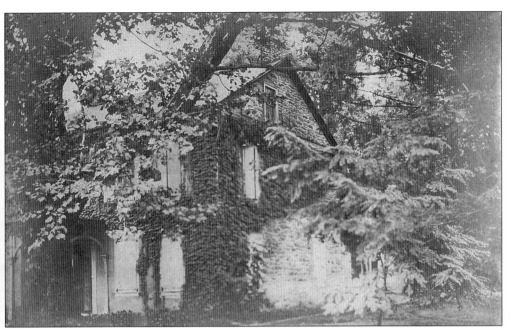

Bernard Reser built Bonneval Cottage around 1735 at the intersection of Old York Road and Oak Lane, then known as Martin's Mill Road. Reser had purchased 78 acres from the Griffith Miles estate. In 1755, Dr. George deBenneville purchased the cottage. DeBenneville was the first resident physician in Milestown. Bonneval Cottage became home to generations of deBennevilles, including Anne deBenneville Mears.

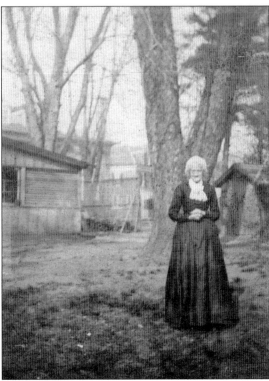

Anne deBenneville Mears (1818–1905) poses in front of one of the many old maple and sycamore trees at Bonneval Cottage. Around 1838, she married Ellwood Mears, a Branchtown neighbor, with whom she had five children. At the age of 31, she became a widow and lived in Bonneval Cottage until her death. She developed into a fine writer, a collector of local tales, and a historian. Her book *Old York Road and its Early Associations* (1890) documents the early history and development of Bristol Township. (GHS.)

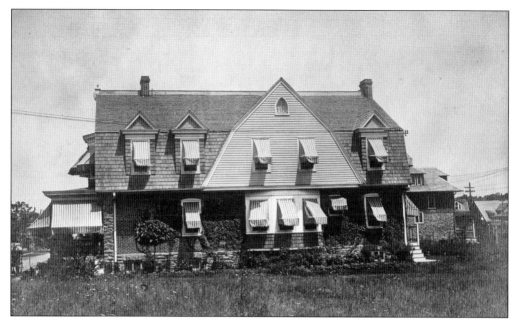

Elizabeth Nothacker lived in her twin, two-and-one-half-story Dutch Revival home at 6415 North Thirteenth Street her entire life. Architect T. Frank Miller (1863–1939) designed this local stone and brick home in the 1920s. Its dormers and bay window covered with wonderful awnings provided a way to keep the home cool in the summer. (Janet McShain.)

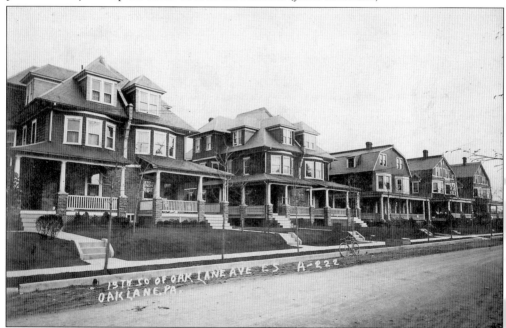

The large twin homes built in the late 1890s on Thirteenth Street, south of Oak Lane, maintain stylistic characteristics in their design elements that make them compatible with the earlier large single homes in East Oak Lane. Colonial Revival or Tudor Revival design elements were incorporated into this more compact housing. After 1950, vernacular houses placed on small lots were built with few design elements but priced affordably. (Andrew M. Herman.)

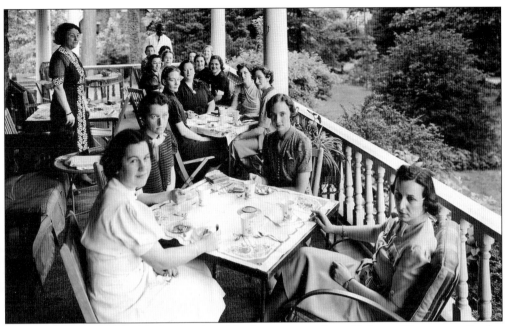

Dr. Albert Fitch (1879–1960), the founder of the Pennsylvania State College of Optometry, lived at 6811 Lawnton Avenue. During World War II, he often hosted luncheons at his home for the female students, as most men were fighting in the war. These women were in the graduating classes of 1940 to 1943 and some lived on the third floor of Fitch's home. Fitch championed the establishment of the optometry profession whose members would be called "Doctor." (Salus University.)

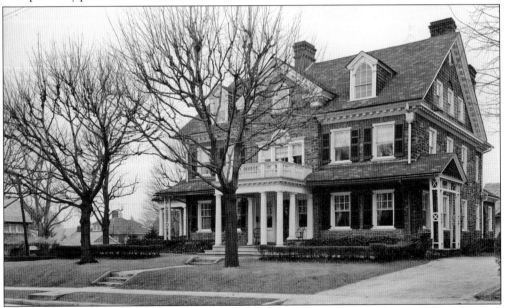

Architect Valentine B. Lee designed a home at 6600 North Eleventh Street for Edward E. Hanscom, who owned Hanscom Brothers Bakery, established in 1883. The three-story mansion has a front that is pure classical revival complete with a Palladian window and classical columns. Lee lived in Oak Lane from 1895 and wrote an essay, "Reminiscences of Early Oak Lane." He designed many mansions in Oak Lane and helped to form the Oak Lane Park Company. (PhillyHistory.)

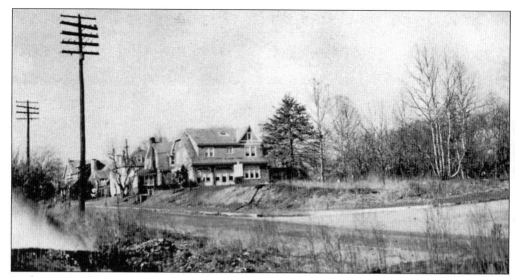

In the 1920s, there were still tracts of undeveloped land in East Oak Lane, such as the land in this photograph that was located at the intersection of Tenth Street and Chelten Avenue. The tracts were purchased by property speculators, such as Edwin Stott. Stott was born in Manchester, England, in 1872. After emigrating, he enrolled in the Frankford Business College. He owned a building and real estate company that bought and sold property in Oak Lane, and he purchased the land between Lawnton Avenue and Tenth Street. He developed the Dutch Colonial home in the foreground, which was built around 1920. (Janet McShain.)

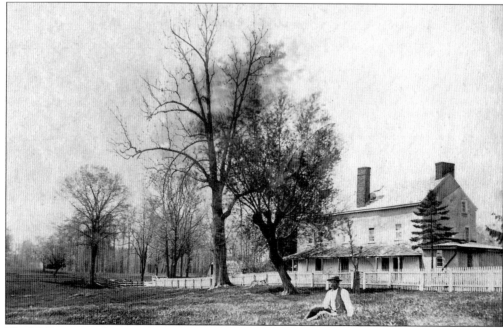

The William Nice farmstead, located in Milestown on some 40 acres that stretched between Oak and Green Lanes east of Old York Road, had been in the family since the late 1700s. The main house was located near the present-day intersection of Eleventh Street and Chelten Avenue. Nice's farm was called Buttonwood, named after a native type of sycamore. The Nice family attended the Milestown Baptist Meeting House and owned and operated the Tavern.

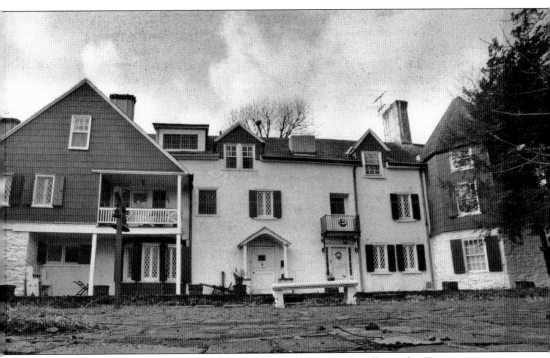

The oldest home in Oak Lane, at 1035 Chelten Avenue, known locally as the Tavern, is more than 300 years old. The 35-room building, equipped with nine fireplaces, sits perpendicular to Chelten Avenue. The first survey of Old York Road, conducted in 1711, makes mention of the tavern, which had a long driveway that originally connected it to the thoroughfare. The Tavern served variously as a resting place for stagecoach travelers, a Quaker meetinghouse, a British outpost during the Revolutionary War, and home to countless families. The octagonal wing of the building likely dates to the late 1700s—the heyday of octagonal building design in America. Kelly McShain Tyree and Devitt McShain currently own the property and have done extensive restoration to the building. They have followed in the footsteps of their great uncle, master builder John McShain (1898–1989). The McShain family has been passionate about Oak Lane history and has championed the neighborhood's beautification. (TUUA.)

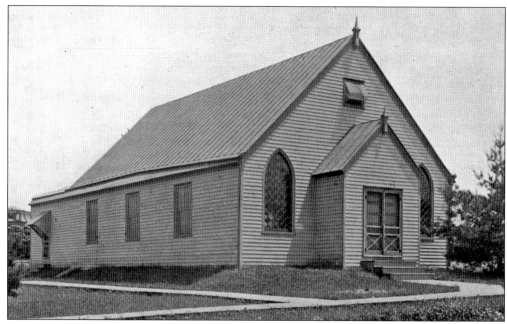

On December 28, 1891, the Oak Lane Presbyterian Church was organized. Shortly thereafter, a lot at the southeast corner of Seventh Street and Sixty-sixth Avenue was chosen for a building site. Charles W. Bolton designed the church, which opened on May 8, 1892. The congregation worshipped here until 1902 when the building was sold to the Reformed Church of Oak Lane. For one year, the Presbyterian congregation held services in Melrose Hall until a new sanctuary at Eleventh Street and Oak Lane was dedicated in 1904. (ATH.)

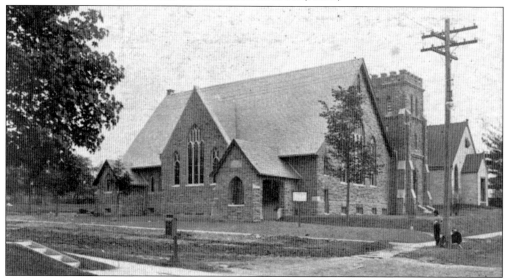

The Reformed Church of Oak Lane was organized, in part, to prevent the sale of the Presbyterian church's property to a developer. The newly formed congregation used the church building for Sunday school classes and erected an adjoining Gothic-style sanctuary in 1905. Valentine B. Lee was the architect. The new building utilized salvaged stone from the Fifth Street Reservoir. The Reformed Church of Oak Lane became the Oak Lane United Church of Christ, which folded in 1984. The 1905 building still stands, while the earlier building was demolished.

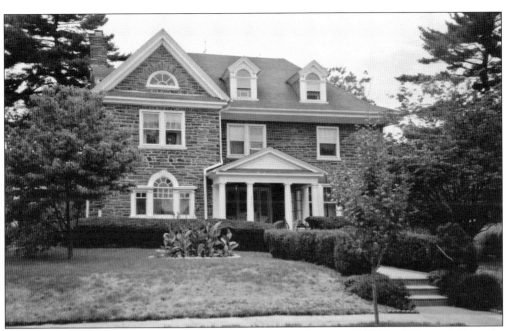

Architect Valentine B. Lee designed the three-story, stone home at 6300 North Seventh Street in 1909. The building was one of Lee's finest Colonial Revival Oak Lane homes and was constructed for George B. Geiser, an inventor with patents for a gutter hanger and snow guard. Lee worked with George O. Lummis, a wealthy land speculator who purchased part of an old estate on which he would build many stately homes in South Oak Lane. (Marita Krivda.)

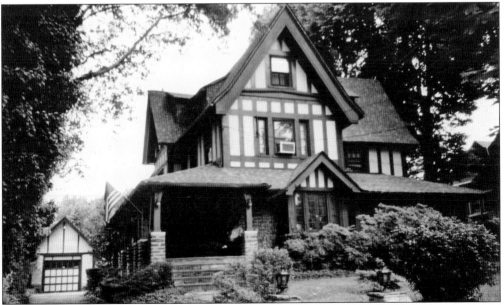

The architectural firm of Lacey and Adams (*fl.* 1908–1909) designed 715 Kenilworth Avenue in 1909 for the Oak Lane Park Building Company. Frank H. Shrenk owned the home for a period in the 1920s. A 1915 advertisement beckoned people to "Come to South Oak Lane; houses and bungalows built to order." The old estates of Edward M. Davis and Harry Ingersoll had been cut up with unpaved streets, and speculators bought lots for suburban residences. (Marita Krivda.)

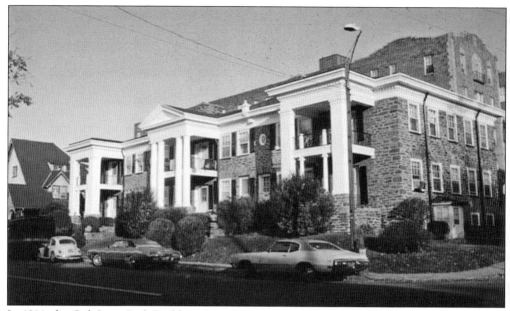

In 1914, the Oak Lane Park Building Company constructed a Colonial Revival-style apartment building at 801–811 Sixty-sixth Avenue, designed by Alexander Mackie Adams (1879–1967). By this time, land speculators had purchased acreage in South Oak Lane from the remaining large estates of Charles H. Fisher, Mary Fox, and David Rorer. In 1912, a developer purchased 8 acres at Eighth Street and Chelten Avenue as a site for costly houses that would sell for $8,000–12,000. (John J. DiBenedetto.)

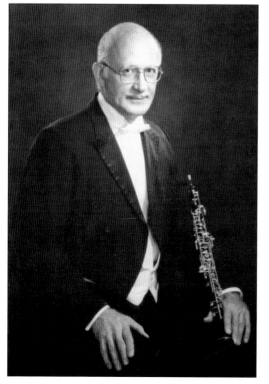

Stevens Hewitt, retired assistant first oboe of the Philadelphia Orchestra, has resided in the Oak Lane Park section of Oak Lane since 1961. Many orchestra colleagues lived nearby. Because of their frequent rehearsals at the Academy of Music, the musicians found the proximity of the subway appealing. Hewitt's neighbors included Anthony Gigliotti (1922–2001), a principal clarinetist in the orchestra, and Louis Rosenblatt (1928–2009), a principal English horn player. (Stevens Hewitt.)

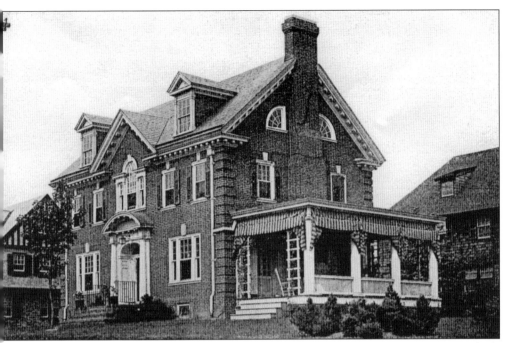

The C. H. Biden Baugh Colonial Revival residence at 6401 North Seventh Street was built in 1913. Baugh was an attorney and vice president of Northern Central Trust Company of Philadelphia. He hired architect William E. Groben to design his home. Groben, also an Oak Lane resident, did preliminary design work for Philadelphia's Benjamin Franklin Parkway, and his wife was active in the suffragist cause. In 1916, she hosted many meetings at their home on Lakeside Avenue. (UPAA.)

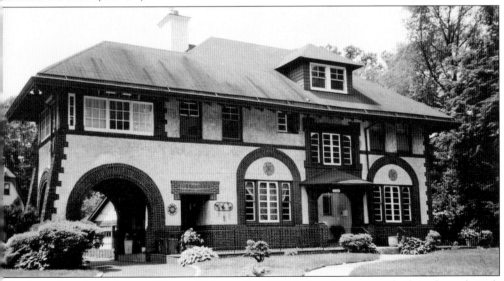

The Spanish-style residence of George O. Lummis at 710 Medary Avenue was built in the early 20th century. Medary and Kenilworth Avenues form a loop containing the grandest of all the Oak Lane Park homes. The Lummis home bears a striking resemblance to the Henry K. Cummings home at 240 West Tulpehocken Street designed by Frank Miles Day (1861–1918). In 1937, Max Bernhardt made alterations to the home for its new owner, Norman S. Rothschild. (Marita Krivda.)

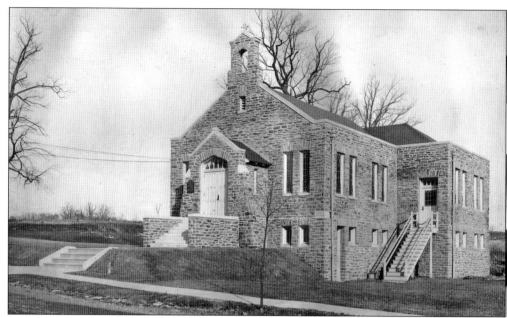

In 1913, Harrison Albright designed a church building for the Oak Lane Park Methodist Episcopal Church and School at 6305 North Sixth Street. In 1930, the church enlarged its sanctuary and adopted a new name, the Bickley Memorial Methodist Episcopal Church, named after George Harvey Bickley (1868–1924), an M. E. bishop from nearby Olney. The church has since been renamed Bickley's New Beginning United Methodist Church. (ATH.)

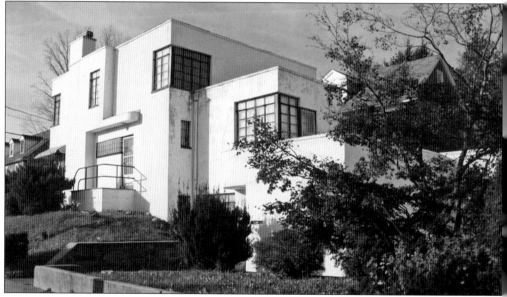

In 1940, Dr. S. Simkins commissioned modernist architect Israel Demchick (1891–1980) to design a home with a professional office at 510 Godfrey Avenue. The result was a masterpiece of Bauhaus architecture. The Bauhaus style, also called the international style, is characterized by a radical simplification of form, a rejection of ornament, and the adoption of glass and concrete as preferred building materials. Scattered throughout East Oak Lane are other Bauhaus-style homes, including the Richard Rose House (1938) and the Leon Sperling House (1936). (David S. Traub.)

Elsie Simonofsky Chomsky and Will Chomsky rented various homes in Oak Lane before purchasing a house at 6417 North Fairhill Street around 1937. There, they raised their two sons, Noam and David (pictured at ages 9 and 4, respectively). Noam went on to be a distinguished linguist and is presently an emeritus professor of linguistics at MIT. His notoriety as a political activist began after the 1969 publication of his book *American Power and the New Mandarins*, which was highly critical of the Vietnam War. (Judith Chomsky.)

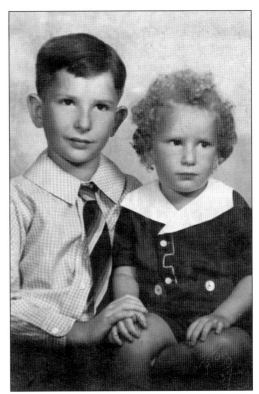

St. Vladimir Ukrainian Orthodox Cathedral stands at North Fifth and Independence Streets. Built in 1966, the architect Nick James Chimes (1924–2002) used Neo-Byzantine architectural elements. The unique umbrella-style roof supports an Orthodox cross and has encircling faceted stained-glass windows at its base. In this photograph, neighbors protest the proposed location of a Fun Bun fast food restaurant across from the church in the mid-1970s. The Fun Bun was built but failed within two years. (TUUA.)

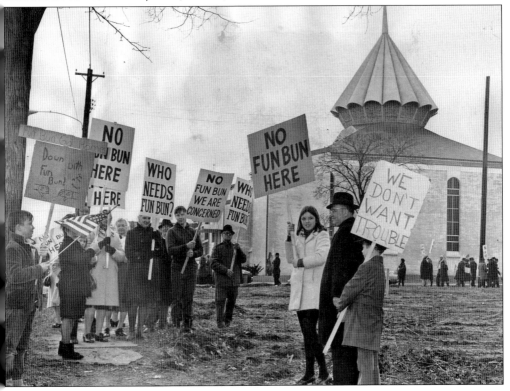

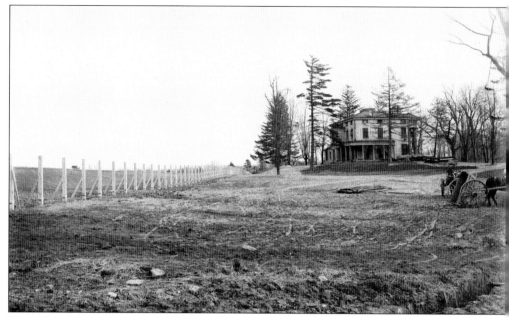

The White Mansion, scheduled for demolition in 1904 to make way for the Oak Lane Reservoir, stood on the hillside near Green Lane. Thomas Griffith owned 100 acres, and in 1770 he sold 50 to Nathan Whitman, who built the White Mansion. As the area grew, the last remaining estates on the eastern edges of Oak Lane were subdivided for housing developments and for the construction of urban infrastructure necessary to sustain the local development. (PhillyHistory.)

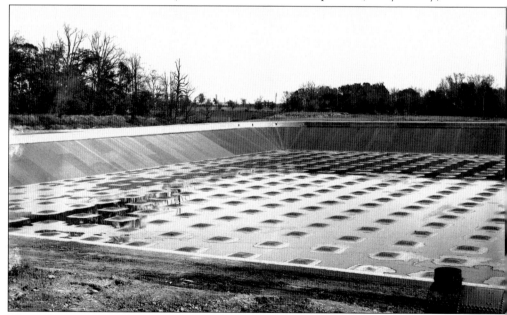

The Oak Lane Reservoir sits on a 21-acre lot between Third and Fifth Streets and Medary and Sixty-fifth Avenues. Designed with two basins and a capacity of 70 million gallons, the reservoir was intended to hold filtered water from the Delaware River. Construction of the reservoir in 1904–1905 was difficult and heavy blasting was necessary. Much of the resulting schist stone was used in the construction of area homes and churches. (PhillyHistory.)

Two

OLNEY

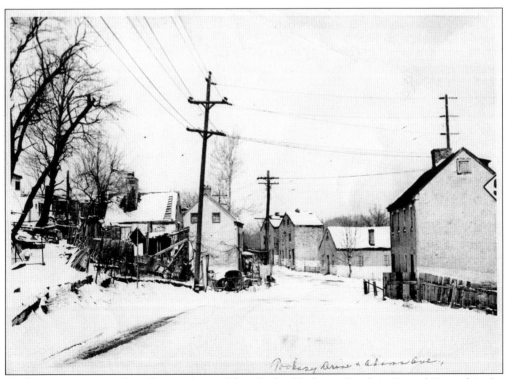

Grubbtown was a small mill town located beside the Tookany Creek in Bristol Township. Its name is connected with the Grubb family of England. Several members of the family lived in and established a grain mill in the area. The Grubbtown buildings at Crescentville Road and Adams Avenue, pictured in the late 1940s, have since been demolished.

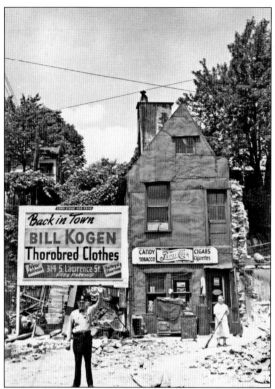

Most Grubbtown buildings, including the house and store pictured, were very modest. One exception was Thomas Griffith's mansion. Griffith, a Quaker, arrived in Philadelphia in 1717 and went on to serve three terms as mayor of Philadelphia (1729–1737). Early maps indicate that his mansion was located on the west bank of the Tookany Creek, and a drawing details its covered porch and several chimneys.

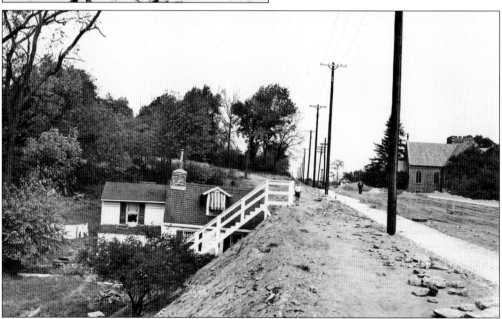

In 1870, Edward Buchanan, brother of Pres. James Buchanan, founded Trinity Chapel. The church was a mission of Trinity Church Oxford, which is still located at Oxford and Longshore Avenues. Trinity Chapel's original building, set on land donated by the Fisher family, was destroyed by fire on November 29, 1925. The chapel was rebuilt in 1927 and can be seen on the far side of Crescentville Road.

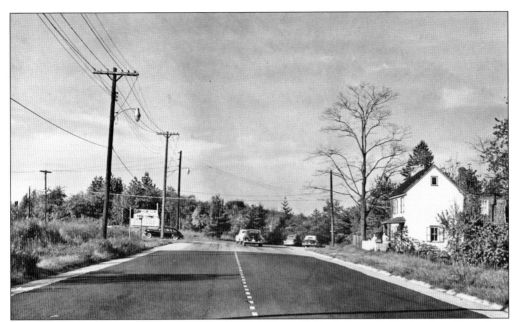

In 1948–1949, Crescentville Road was paved and extended north through Cheltenham Township. The extension, named the Tookany Creek Parkway, follows the Tookany/Tacony Creek. The delineation between Crescentville Road and Tookany Creek Parkway, which occurs at Cheltenham Avenue, is visible in this image. The creek is surrounded by 130 acres of park and diverse wildlife. Currently, it is being championed by the Tookany/Tacony-Frankford Watershed Partnership.

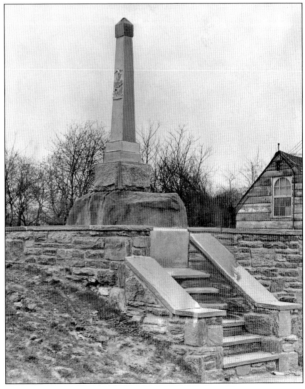

A marble and granite monument, located in the Olney Recreation Center at A Street and Champlost Avenue, honors the men of Grubbtown who fought in the Civil War. It reads, "More men went to war from this village than any other similar town in the United States." According to local legend, all able-bodied men from Grubbtown, save one, chose to fight for the Union. The abstainer was tarred and feathered and thrown into the Tacony Creek by the local housewives. The monument was dedicated on July 4, 1899, and was restored in 1998. (TUUA.)

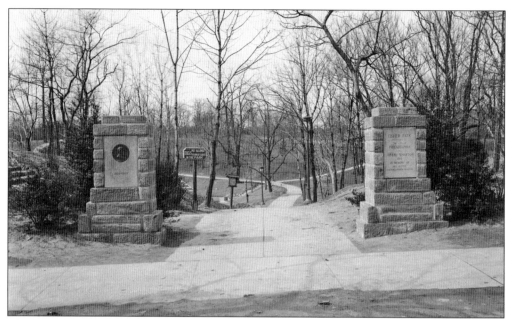

The main entrance to Fisher Park is located at Fifth and Fern Streets. The 23-acre park was donated to the City of Philadelphia by Joseph Wharton in 1908. Wharton (1826–1909) is remembered for his industrial and philanthropic accomplishments, which include cofounding the Bethlehem Steel Company, founding the Wharton School of the University of Pennsylvania, and cofounding Swarthmore College. (PhillyHistory.)

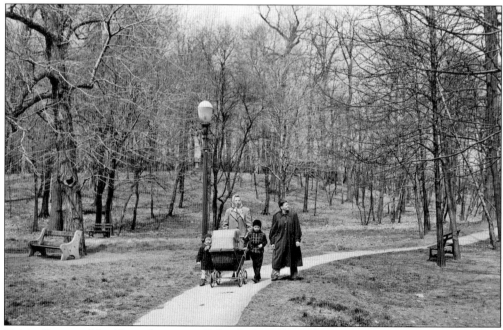

Originally part of the Champlost estate, Fisher Park is Olney's largest park. Prior to the construction of a sewer in 1922, Rock Run Creek, a tributary of Tacony Creek, traversed the park. Currently, the park contains a recreation center, a playground, basketball and tennis courts, a football field, and hiking trails. (TUUA.)

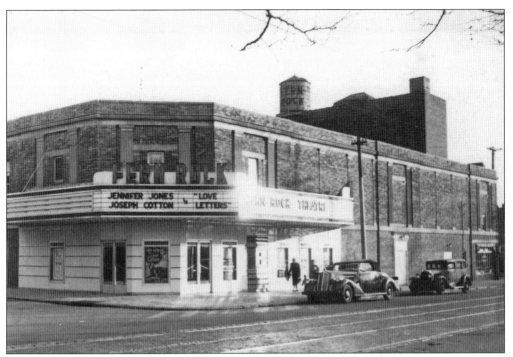

The Fern Rock Theatre, which was located at 6017 North Fifth Street, was built in 1928. It was designed by the firm of Hodgens and Hill (*fl.* 1923–1942) and accommodated up to 1,289 patrons. The interior featured an asbestos curtain, a decorated proscenium arch, and ornate organ grilles. Originally an RKO-Stanley Warner theater, it was acquired by the Sameric Corporation in the 1970s. It remained open until the late 1980s. The building still stands and is now a market and dollar store. (Both, ATH.)

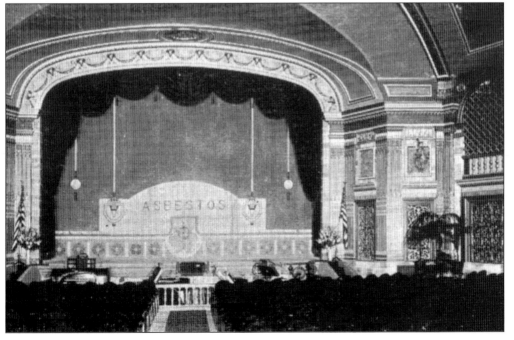

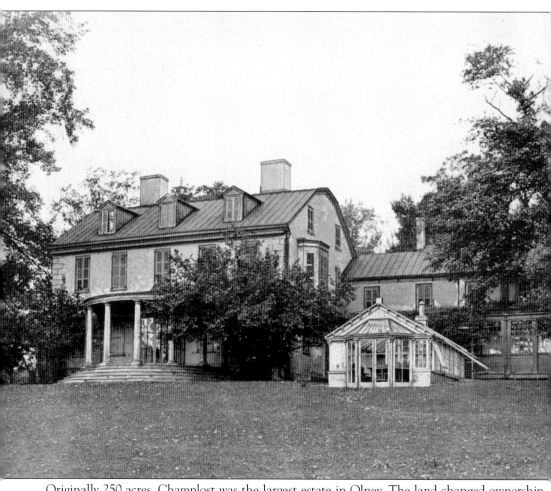

Originally 250 acres, Champlost was the largest estate in Olney. The land changed ownership three times before 1909. William Penn, John Worrell, and James Porteus jointly owned the land before it passed to Joseph Fox and Edward Warner in 1737. In 1770, Joseph Fox erected the main house. The Fox family retained Champlost until Mary Dickinson Fox died in 1895. After her death, the main house and farm buildings, which were concentrated around Fifth Street and Champlost Street, were neglected. In 1904, Joseph Wharton purchased a 120-acre portion of the estate, and in 1907, the City considered purchasing and incorporating the remaining 69 acres into Fairmount Park. Instead, in 1909 the remaining acres were sold to developer Harry Schmitt for $260,000. Subsequently, Schmitt demolished the mansion and erected several hundred houses between Nedro Avenue, Tabor Road, Sixth Street, and the North Pennsylvania Railroad tracks.

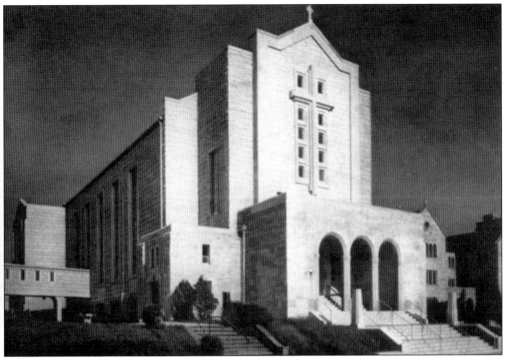

St. Helena's Parish was founded in 1924 by Fr. James McCloy. The first mass was celebrated at St. Stephen's Church at Broad and Butler Streets and subsequent masses were held in a private home and the Olney Theatre. In 1926, St. Helena's moved into a new building at Fifth and Spencer Streets. The chapel (pictured above) was erected in 1950. The structure was designed by Gleeson and Mulrooney (*fl.* 1924–1958). It features marble work by the Lorenzoni Company, intricate stained-glass windows, and mosaics. (PAHRC.)

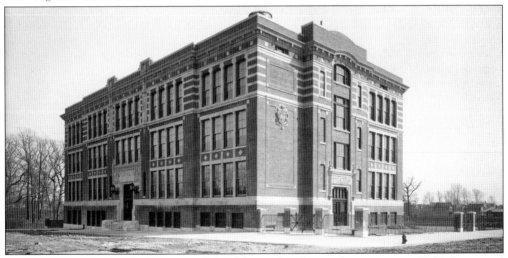

The James Russell Lowell Elementary School, located at the northwest corner of Fifth Street and Nedro Avenue, was completed in 1914. The building was designed by H. DeCourcey Richards (*fl.* 1906–1923). In 1951, resident and merchant William R. Hess recalled that the school "was the first modern school in this section. When they built it, the parents complained that their kids had to wade through mud to get to school. That's how things were then." (PhillyHistory.)

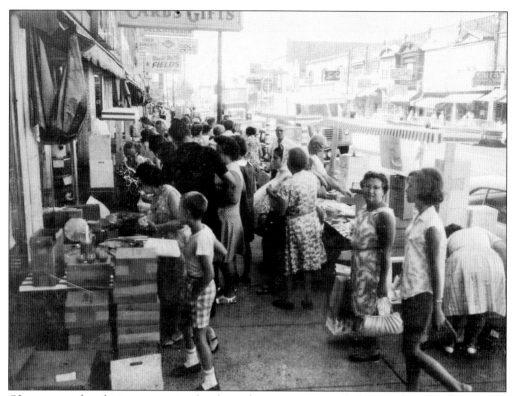

Olney was a close-knit community that hosted many events, including a sidewalk sale. In 1951, Olney resident and librarian Anne Strykowski said, "The nicest thing here is the grand community spirit. I never saw anything like it anywhere else. It affords a great many contacts outside the home. Symphony concerts and musical plays at the high school auditorium, for instance. You get to know your neighbors. I think outside activities are good because they help make good citizens."

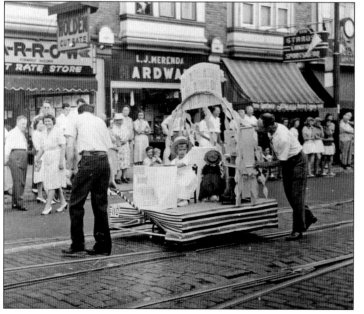

During Olney's heyday, nearly all of the community participated in the Fourth of July festivities. Typically the day's events included a parade, speeches, music, dancing, and fireworks at Olney High School. The highlight of the celebration was the baby parade for boys and girls under the age of six. The costumed children rode or walked north on Fifth Street, beginning at Tabor Road and ending at Lowell Elementary School.

The *Olney Times* newspaper, which was founded in 1909, was published weekly for nearly 100 years. Thomas F. Reilly, dubbed "The Voice of Olney" by neighbors, owned, edited, and published the paper for many years until his death on December 6, 1996. The paper was later sold to the Journal Register Company (JRC). On December 11, 2008, the JRC shut down the *Olney Times* along with the *Northeast News Gleaner* and the *Northeast Breeze*.

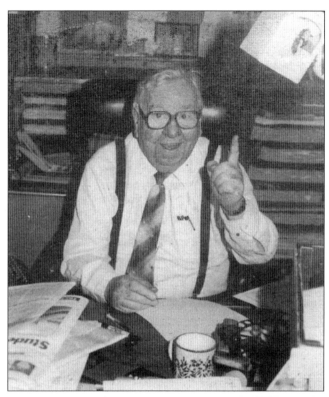

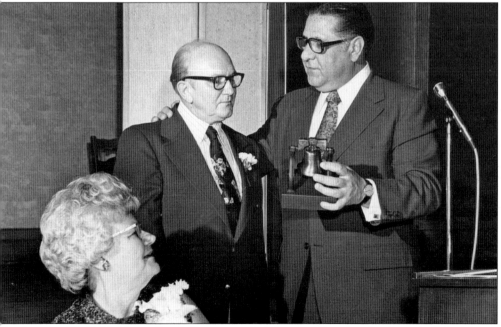

On January 23, 1975, Mayor Frank Rizzo awarded Eugene Mansdoerfer the title "Mr. Olney." Mansdoerfer loved and invested in his neighborhood. He volunteered for many community civic associations, the schools, and the churches. He directed the Greater Olney Civic Association's Fourth of July celebration and served as a scoutmaster in the Boy Scouts for more than 50 years.

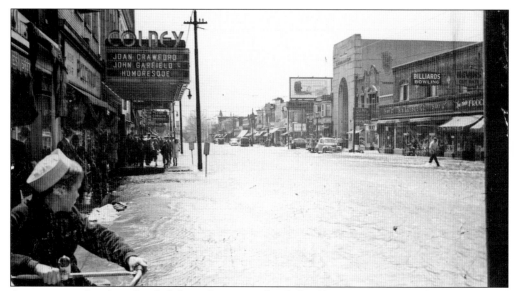

A water main break at the Oak Lane Reservoir flooded Fifth Street in 1948. The water flowed down Fifth Street until navy divers were able to locate and fix the break. In its prime, this stretch of Fifth Street, between Chew and Olney Avenues, boasted a department store, clothing stores, shoe stores, restaurants, four delicatessens, four bakeries, and an ice cream parlor.

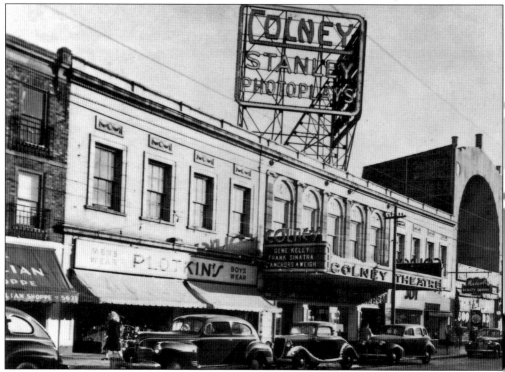

The Colney Theatre, completed in 1924, was designed by Hodgens and Hill, who also designed the Fern Rock Theatre. The popular movie theater was located at 5621–5629 North Fifth Street, near the hub of Olney's commercial district. It accommodated up to 1,985 patrons. The theater closed in 1958, and the extant building was divided into several stores. (ATH.)

In 1965, the Girard Trust Company purchased a bank building at 5604–5606 North Fifth Street from the Fidelity-Philadelphia Trust Company for $112,000. After extensive alterations, it was reopened as the Girard Trust Company's Olney branch. Recently, the North Fifth Street Revitalization Project partnered with the building's current owner to remove architecturally dissonant signage and to improve the appearance of the structure.

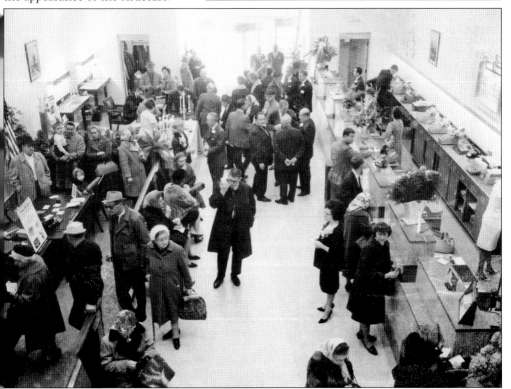

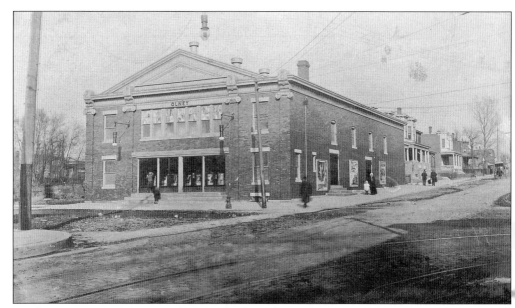

Frank Hess's "moving pictures" theater, which was located at the northeast corner of Fifth Street and Olney Avenue, was built sometime between 1910 and 1913. At that time, it was the only structure on the block. St. Helena's Parish held Mass here from 1924 to 1926. William B. Mooney provided music for both the silent films and the masses. The theater was demolished sometime in the 1930s. (Andrew M. Herman.)

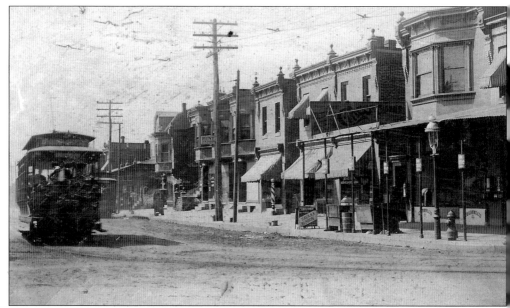

Today the intersection of Fifth Street and Olney Avenue is considered the heart of Olney. In this view from the early 1900s looking south, O'Donnell's Cigar and Candy Store and Baker's Pharmacy are visible in the foreground. The trolley tracks guided the Route 75 trolley, which traveled north from Fifth Street and Wyoming Avenue to Germantown.

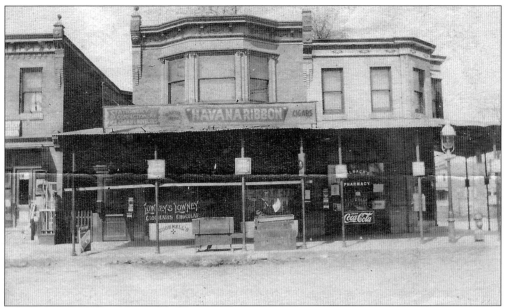

O'Donnell's Cigar and Candy Store and Baker's Pharmacy were located at the southwest corner of Fifth Street and Olney Avenue. Residents recall there was a billiard room in the basement of O'Donnell's. Both buildings are still standing but barely recognizable.

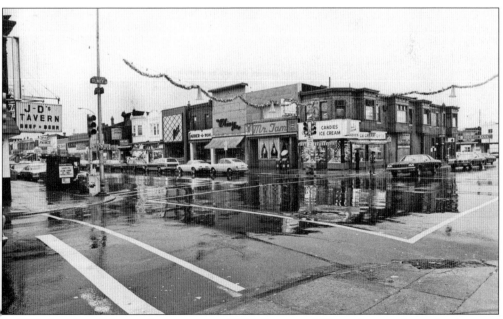

In 1977, the view of the southwest corner of Fifth Street and Olney Avenue shows the degree of change that had occurred. The second floor of the corner building is familiar, but the majority of the block has been significantly altered. Founded in 2005, the North Fifth Street Revitalization Project partnered with local businesses, the Greater Olney Branch of the Free Library of Philadelphia, and neighborhood residents to improve the appearance and safety of North Fifth Street. (TUUA.)

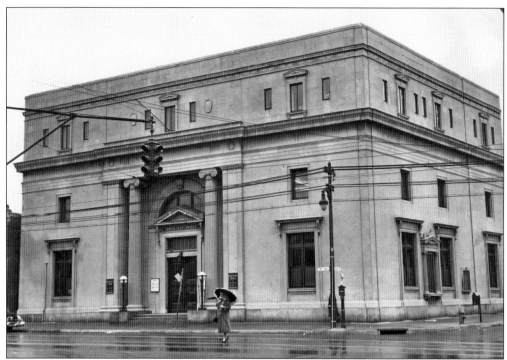

The Greater Olney Branch of the Free Library of Philadelphia opened in 1949 at the northeast corner of Fifth Street and Tabor Road. Before serving the community as a library, the building housed the Olney Bank and Trust Company. Previously, the library was located at B and Lima Streets, then Rising Sun Avenue and Tabor Road. The extant building still houses the library and was renovated in 1997. (TUUA.)

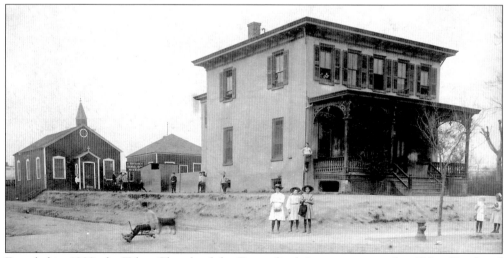

Founded in 1908, the Tabor Church of the Evangelical Association stood at Tabor Road and Lawrence Street. The German church owned the entire corner site, occupying the modest chapel and adjoining building, while renting the corner home to the Olney Public School because it required additional space. Later the congregation reorganized as the Salem Evangelical Church and moved to Chew and Lawrence Streets. Eventually, Olney Federal Savings and Loan replaced these buildings. (Andrew M. Herman.)

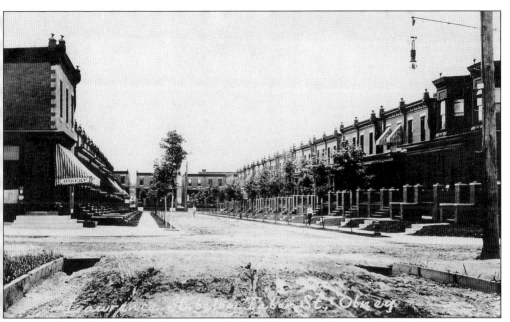

Lawrence Street, below Tabor Street, was developed sometime between 1906 and 1910. The row houses still stand, although they are missing their distinctive architectural details and have gained stucco and siding, typically added to reduce the cost of upkeep.

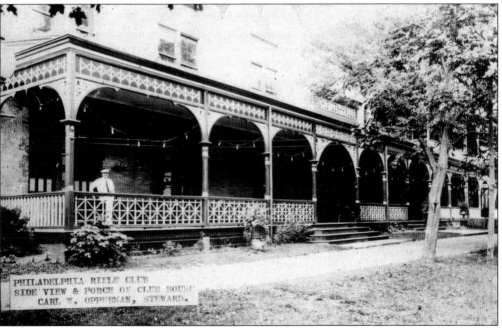

The Philadelphia Rifle Club, a prominent German club, was founded in 1846. In 1893, the club purchased 10 acres of ground from Peter C. Hollis on which they built a new clubhouse. Opened in 1895, the building was located near Eighth Street and Tabor Road and contained reception and dining rooms, a kitchen, card rooms, and a large dancing hall. The club held an annual meeting and weekly shooting competitions. Though the organization is now defunct, the clubhouse building still stands. (Robert M. Skaler.)

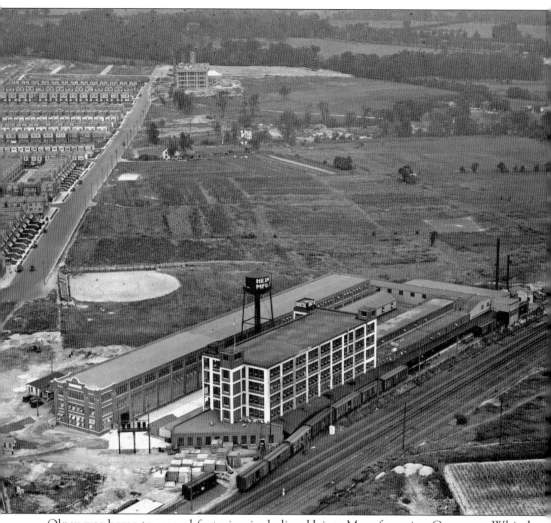

Olney was home to several factories, including Heintz Manufacturing Company, Whitaker Mills, Proctor and Schwartz, the Olney Foundry, and the Germantown Tool Works. The Heintz Manufacturing Company was founded by Leo Heintz in 1921. The plant, located at Front Street and Olney Avenue, was situated on 33 acres. Heintz produced metal items such as sink basins, soft drink bottle dispensers, and stainless steel cabs for trains. Following the death of Heintz in 1932, the company hired William Meinel from the Budd Company as president, a position he held for 20 years. In 1958, Heintz was sold to Kelsey-Hayes Corporation, which has since been through many mergers and acquisitions. Heintz has remained a division of the parent company ever since. The company remained in Olney until 1985. At that time, the plant was demolished and replaced with the One and Olney strip mall, which subsequently siphoned business from Olney's small businesses along Fifth Street. The Thomas K. Finletter School is under construction in the distance. (LCP.)

During World War II, the Heintz Manufacturing Company produced machine guns, rocket launchers, and other war products. On August 19, 1942, the employees gathered for a rally featuring an ordnance display and pep talk. Several local children perched atop the wall to have a look for themselves. (TUUA.)

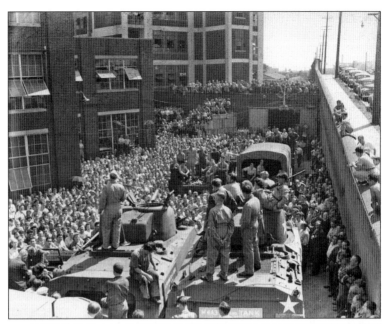

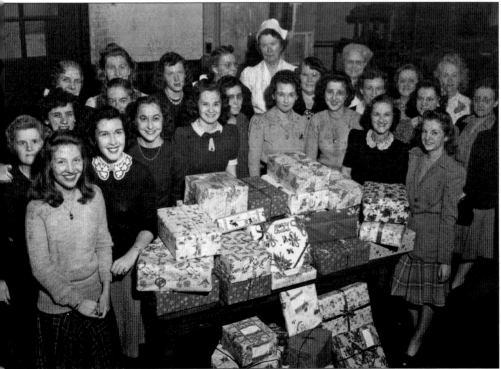

The ladies of Proctor and Schwartz, which produced textile machinery at Seventh Street and Tabor Road, gifted items to "unknown soldiers" for Christmas in 1942. Ruth Baus conceived the idea to send gifts to Fort Knox, Kentucky, after her fiancé told her that many soldiers rarely receive letters and never receive packages. Thirty-four women assembled about 50 packages that contained items such as shoe polish, socks, toothbrushes, toothpaste, cookies, candy, and playing cards. (TUUA.)

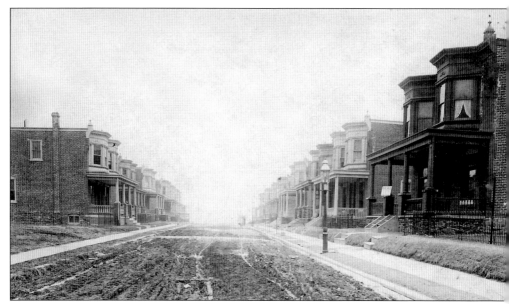

Wentz Street, looking east from Mascher Street, sported neat row houses. The houses on the south side were erected on the former Jonah Wentz estate and were built sometime between 1910 and 1913. The houses on the north side were erected by 1923, on the former Margaret Felton estate, which was bounded by Chew Avenue and Front, Wentz, and Mascher Streets. (Andrew M. Herman.)

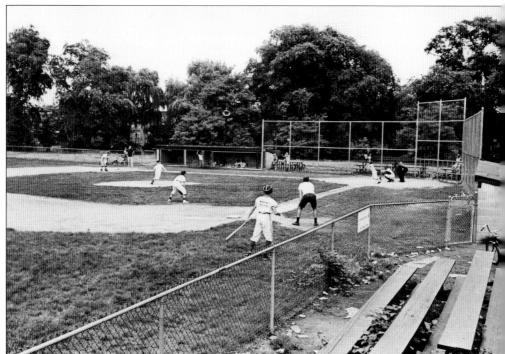

The Kiwanis Field, located at B Street and Olney Avenue, has hosted baseball games for many years. The teams of the Olney Midget Baseball League were named after the major league teams. Playing on July 17, 1967, were the Phils and the Orioles. (TUUA.)

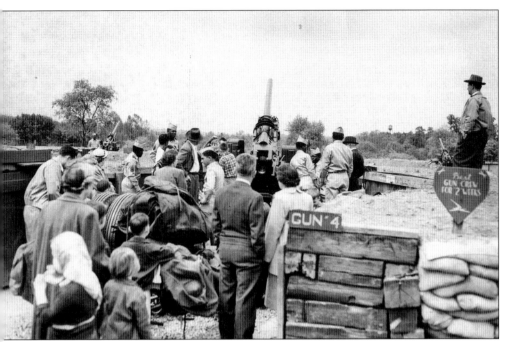

In the late 1950s, soldiers and radar operators monitored the skies above Rising Sun and Olney Avenues. They were equipped with cannons designed to destroy enemy aircraft. The operation was closed in 1959, when the army obtained new Nike missiles. Once dotted with buildings and artillery, nature has since reclaimed the site.

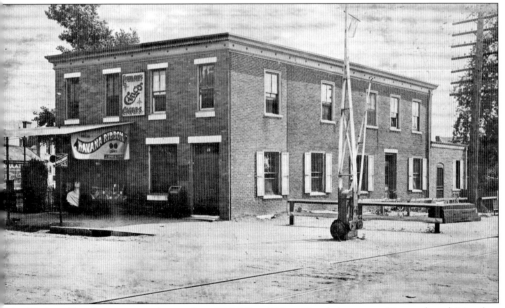

The Philips Candy store was located at 136 West Tabor Road, between Howard and Mascher Streets. The store boasted an extensive selection of penny candies and also served as Olney's post office. Just outside the store, the Reading Railroad tracks crossed the road. Sometime between 1907 and 1914, the railroad elevated and widened the tracks to increase capacity and to ensure safety in the growing neighborhood.

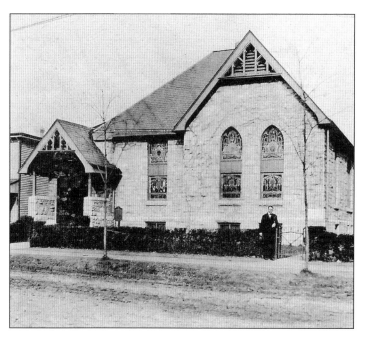

The First Presbyterian Church of Olney, located at Third Street and Tabor Road, was founded in 1898. In 1903, the main sanctuary was built. This structure was replaced in 1926 by a larger sanctuary, which still stands. In 1917, a Sunday school was constructed at Third Street and Clarkson Avenue. The church was founded by the Reverend William Henry Wells with 51 members. By the time the Sunday school was completed, the church had 764 members. (Andrew M. Herman.)

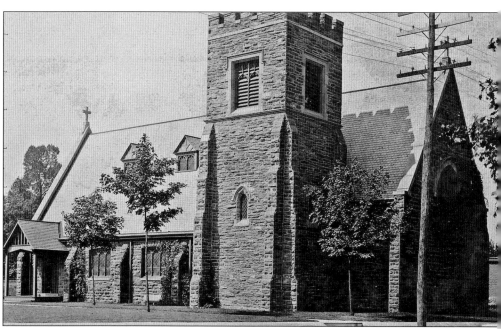

In 1891, the Episcopal Convocation of Germantown planted a mission church in Olney. The Reverend Dr. Samuel Upjohn was the founding minister, and the congregation originally met at Rising Sun Avenue and Tabor Road. Architect George T. Pearson (1847–1920) designed an English Gothic church building that was constructed in 1897 at Second Street and Tabor Road for the congregation of St. Alban's. In 1914, the Reverend Archibald Knowles, the church's second rector, hired Pearson to enlarge the sanctuary as a memorial to his father, George Lambert Knowles. The earlier buildings were largely pulled down to make way for the new buildings. (Andrew M. Herman.)

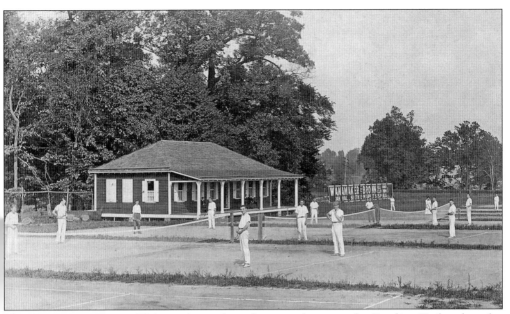

The Greenpoint Tennis Club was located on the green between the Reading Railroad tracks, Front Street, and Tabor Road. Additional tennis clubs in Olney were the Olney Tennis Club and the Philadelphia and Reading Athletic Club. The Greenpoint and P and R Clubs were members of the Suburban Tennis League. Greenpoint Tennis Club was active from before 1910 into the 1920s and won the league championship several times. (Andrew M. Herman.)

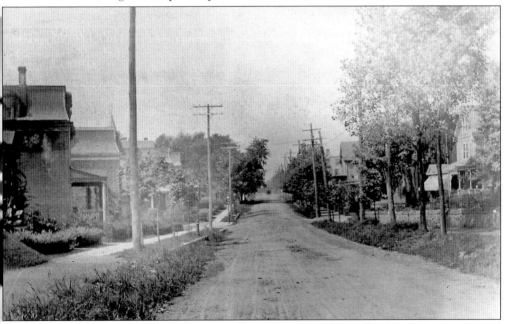

The oldest and largest houses in Olney were still standing in 1906 on Tabor Road, between Second and Mascher Streets. The Philadelphia Court of Quarter Sessions laid out Tabor Road (formerly Olney Road) in 1776 to connect Germantown to Trinity Church, at Disston Street and Oxford Avenue. This area was called Wentzville, after the Wentz family of Germany. Several of these houses still stand. (Andrew M. Herman.)

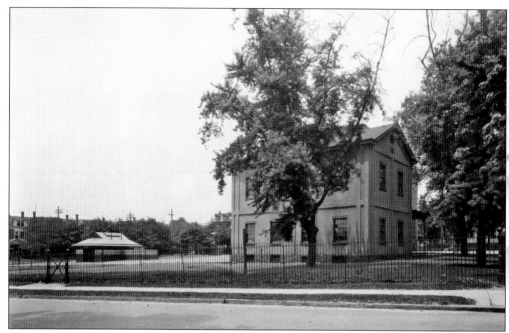

Olney's first school, which opened September 29, 1849, consisted of two rooms, a detached toilet, and stove heater. The building was made of wood and roughcast brick with a shingle roof and was located at the southeast corner of Tabor Road and Water Street. In 1882, it was enlarged and improved, receiving a second floor with two rooms and a new heating system. (PhillyHistory.)

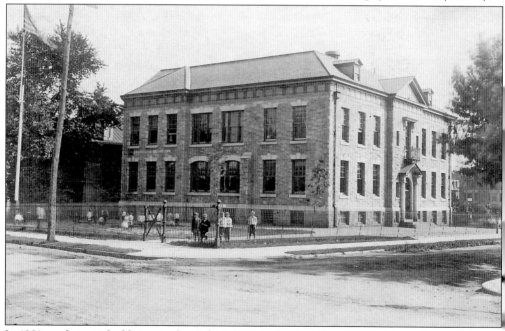

In 1901, a substantial addition in the Colonial Revival style designed by architect Andrew J. Sauer (1880–1940) was added to the 1882 school building. In 1926, the school was expanded again, but this time the plans called for razing the old structure. The new building still stands as the Olney Elementary School. (Andrew M. Herman.)

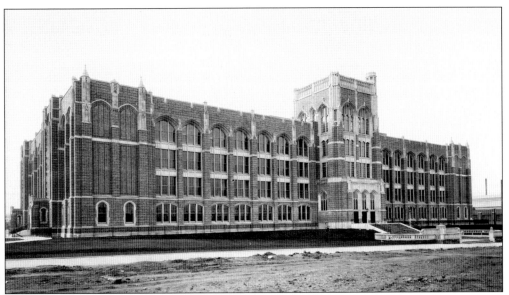

Olney High School, completed in 1931, was designed by Philadelphia architect Irwin T. Catharine (1884–1944). Catharine designed many Philadelphia public schools, including Masterman Laboratory and Demonstration School and Central High School. Notable Olney alumni include Phillies outfielder Del Ennis (class of 1942), writer Barry S. Waronker (class of 1965), and television reporter Sheila Washington (class of 1982). (PhillyHistory.)

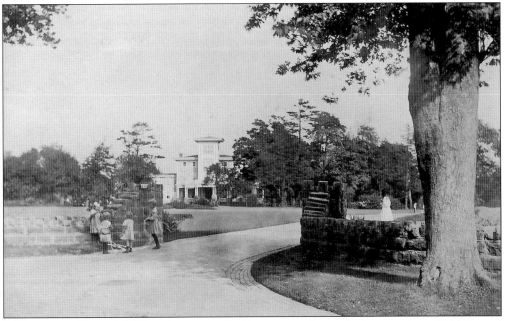

William Burk (1848–1907) lived in a grand Italianate mansion at the intersection of Old Second Street Pike and Tabor Road. The house was considered "among the finest of the section." Burk was the founder of William Burk and Brother, a wholesale butcher and pork packing establishment that was located on North Third Street. He and his brothers were involved in various meat processing businesses and his one brother Henry went on to become a congressman. The house no longer stands. (Andrew M. Herman.)

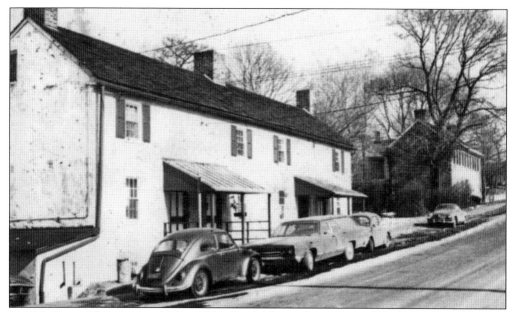

In 1813, Henry Whitaker established Whitaker Mills on the east side of Tookany Creek, between Rising Sun Avenue and Whitaker Avenue. Originally the site consisted of 40 acres of land, 20 houses, and a cotton factory. Eventually the mill expanded to the west side of the creek. The Whitaker family maintained ownership and operation of the business until 1973. In 1977, Howard Whitaker donated the buildings pictured above and 2 acres of land to the city. The buildings have since been demolished.

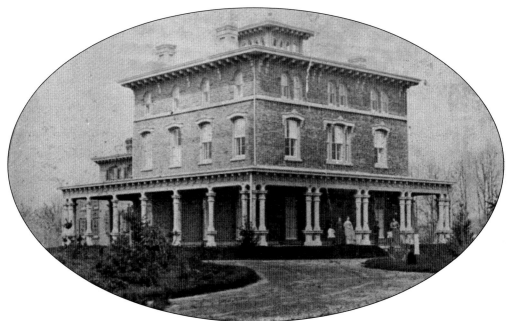

Henry Whitaker's son, William, built an Italianate mansion at the southwest corner of Adams Avenue and Tabor Road, just beyond Olney's eastern boundary. In 1921, Ann Whitaker died, and the 83-acre estate was sold at auction. Today a McDonald's restaurant and a bank occupy the site.

Three

LOGAN

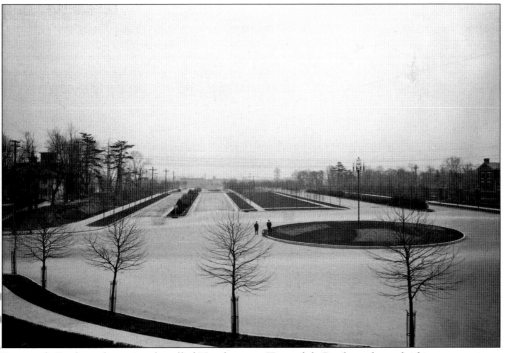

Roosevelt Boulevard, previously called Northeast or Torresdale Boulevard, was laid in two sections. The first stretched from Broad Street to Cayuga Street, and the second stretched to the Pennypack Creek. The two sections were completed in 1913 and 1914, respectively, and the road terminated at Broad Street in a large traffic circle (pictured). The current name of the highway honors Pres. Theodore Roosevelt. (PhillyHistory.)

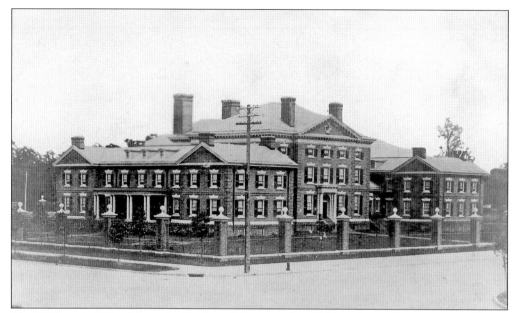

The William L. Elkins Home for Orphan Girls opened in 1904 at the southeast corner of Broad Street and the Roosevelt Boulevard. The brick building, which was designed by Philadelphia architect Horace Trumbauer (1868–1938), contained offices, classrooms, libraries, and dormitories. Currently the building is owned by the Prince Hall Grand Lodge of Pennsylvania.

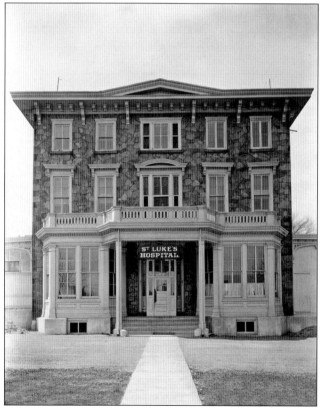

St. Luke's Hospital opened on January 9, 1896. Originally housed in a private dwelling at 3318 North Broad Street, it moved into this building at Broad and Wingohocking Streets in 1904. The hospital remained here until 1927 when it merged with the Children's Homeopathic Hospital. At that time, the newly formed St. Luke's and Children's Medical Center relocated to Eighth and Thompson Streets. The building at Broad and Wingohocking Streets has been demolished. (PhillyHistory.)

The southeast section of Logan was developed in the early 20th century. The neighborhood primarily consisted of Wissahickon schist and brick row houses, and the streets were lined with sycamore trees. The house pictured was located at 1015 West Wingohocking Street. (PhillyHistory.)

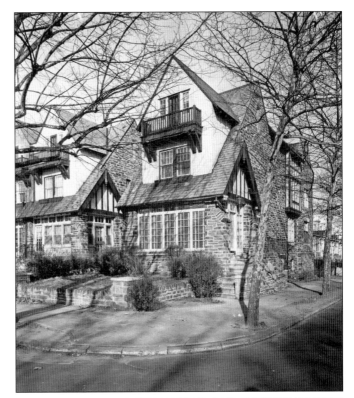

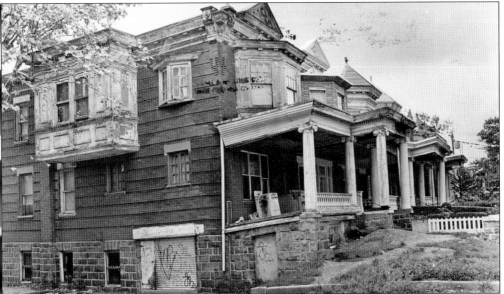

Shortly after their completion, the houses in the southeast section of Logan began sinking. Their settling foundations caused dangerous collapses and gas leaks. Eventually the residents learned that their homes were built on coal ash, which had been dumped along the buried Wingohocking Creek. In the mid-1980s, after much legal wrangling, the houses were demolished. Today the 35-acre Logan Triangle remains undeveloped. Pictured above is the 800 block of Wyoming Street prior to demolition. (FLP.)

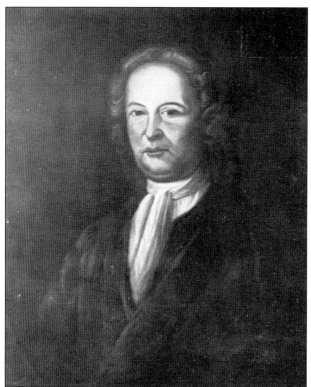

James Logan was born in Lurgan, Ireland, in 1674. While serving as master of the Friar Meetinghouse School, Logan became acquainted with board member William Penn. In 1699, Penn invited Logan to accompany him to America to serve as his secretary. Logan's official appointments included commissioner of property (1701), receiver general (1701), clerk of the provincial council (1701), mayor of Philadelphia (1723), and chief justice of the Pennsylvania Supreme Court (1726).

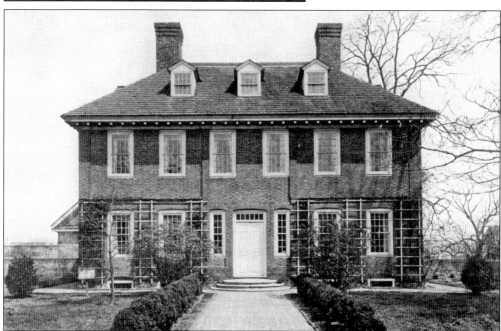

A Quaker like Penn, Logan became wealthy by investing in land, trading furs, and shipping goods to the Mediterranean region, the Carolinas, and Newfoundland. In 1726, he built his mansion, Stenton, where he entertained guests and engaged in scholarly pursuits. Logan experimented with plants and wrote articles about botany, astronomy, and mathematics. (FLP.)

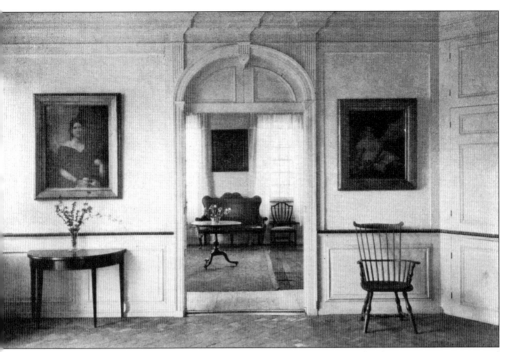

The interior of Stenton features wood paneling and fine furniture. The furniture was imported from England or was built by the best cabinet makers in America. Stenton still stands in Stenton Park at Sixteenth Street and Wyoming Avenue. The room interiors remain virtually untouched and most of the furniture is original. (FLP.)

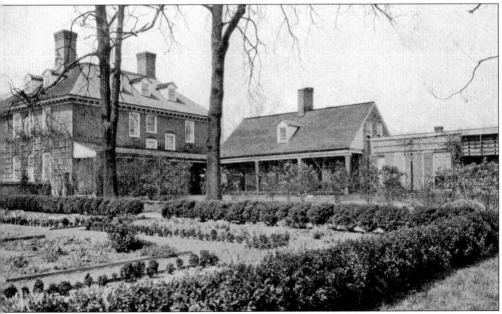

Stenton is an outstanding and rare example of Georgian architecture. The facade is brick with Flemish bond work and pilasters. The sides and back are not symmetrical. In 1899, the Colonial Dames of America obtained the property and have maintained it as a house museum since then. (FLP.)

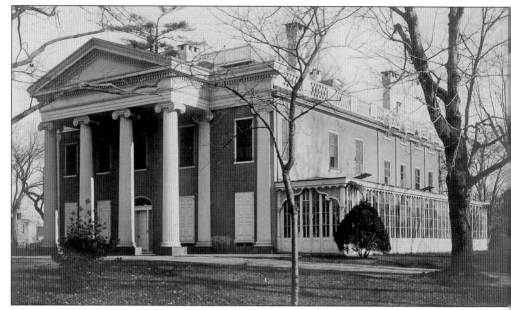

The residence of J. Bertram Lippincott was located at the southeast corner of Old York Road and Wyoming Avenue. Lippincott was the third president of the publishing firm J. B. Lippincott and Company. The mansion was built by a Mr. Hanson and was enlarged by Lippincott's wife's grandfather, Mr. Lovering, a sugar manufacturer. The ground had originally been part of the Solitude estate. The house was eventually demolished and is the present location of a Burger King. (Andrew M. Herman.)

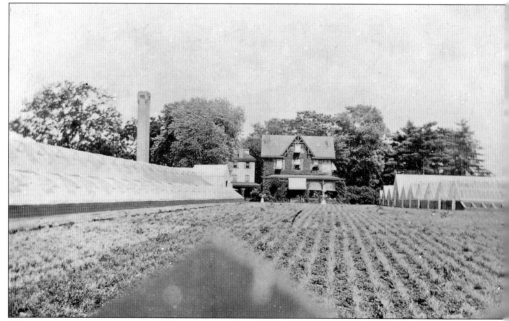

The A. P. Irwin Nursery was located at Broad and Loudon Streets in 1896. The Irwin Nursery was the only nursery in the area, although a former nurseryman had operated on this site in the 1880s and florist Hugh Graham owned the property in 1892. Today this stretch of Broad Street is densely populated by small businesses and apartments.

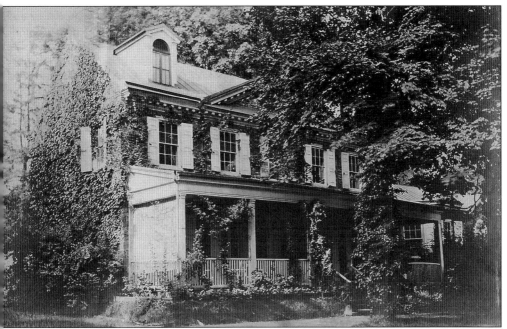

John Roberts built Solitude for his daughter, Sarah, in 1775. Sarah married David Evans, who owned a cabinet and undertaking business at Sixth and Arch Streets. During the Battle of Germantown on October 4, 1777, Gen. Charles Cornwallis inhabited the farmhouse, and his soldiers operated a hospital in the main building. Casualties were buried in a large vault on the property.

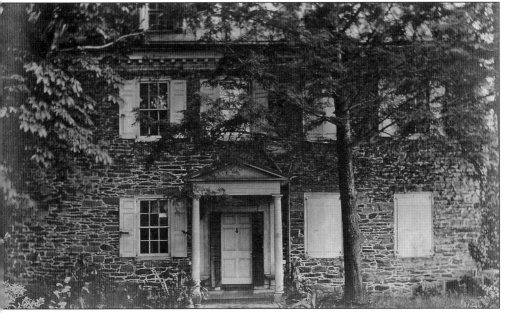

Solitude was the centerpiece of an 80-acre estate located east of Old York Road, between Fishers Lane and the Wingohocking Creek. The main house featured high mantels, open fireplaces, and carved woodwork. After 1799, the estate changed hands many times. In 1903, a syndicate headed by John C. Bell purchased the estate for $285,000. Subsequently, they demolished the buildings (including three houses and several barns), leveled the trees, and developed the area.

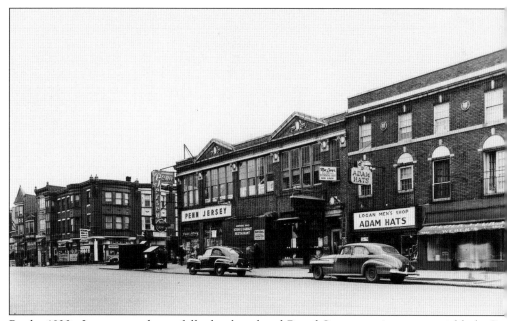

By the 1930s, Logan was almost fully developed and Broad Street was its commercial hub. On Broad Street, between Louden and Ruscomb Streets, stood a variety of stores, the Bell Telephone Building, and the Rockland Theatre. A luncheonette and pharmacy, a Penn Jersey Auto Store, Horn and Hardart Restaurant, Mac Levy's Slendering Salon, Adam Hats, and Weber's Furs are visible in this 1950s view of the southeast corner of Broad and Rockland Streets.

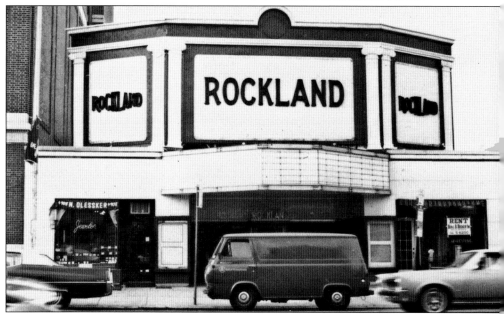

The Rockland Theatre opened in 1914 at 4910 North Broad Street. The eclectic building was designed by Albert F. Schenck (1877–1931). It was later altered by the Hoffman-Henon Company (fl. 1918-1930), which designed a number of theaters, including the Boyd Theatre at Nineteenth and Chestnut Streets in Center City. The Rockland Theatre could accommodate up to 850 moviegoers. It was demolished in 1970. (ATH.)

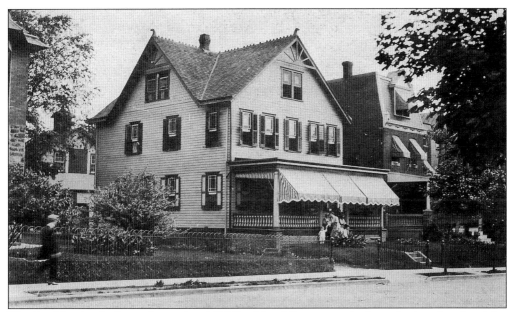

The Rockland, which was located at 1308 Rockland Street, was built in the last decade of the nineteenth century. It, and many other homes like it, was erected by the Logan Real Estate Company. Today the site is occupied by a small apartment building. (Andrew M. Herman.)

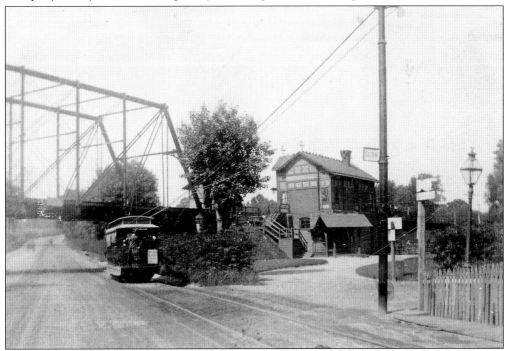

The Philadelphia and Reading Railroad was chartered in 1833 to transport coal from eastern Pennsylvania to Philadelphia. The main line ran through Tabor to Center City. On October 6, 1879, the Tabor Branch of the railroad opened, connecting Wayne Junction with Tabor and crossing Broad Street at Logan. The Logan Station was located at the northeast corner of Old York Road and Fishers Lane. This building was replaced in 1911.

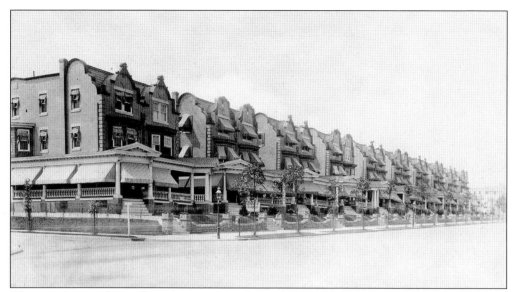

The twin houses, located on the east side of Broad Street between Duncannon and Lindley Avenues, were erected sometime between 1906 and 1910. The land was sold by Mary R. Fox, and the 20 identical houses were built by Edward S. Radley of the Broad Street National Bank. All of the houses are extant. (Andrew M. Herman.)

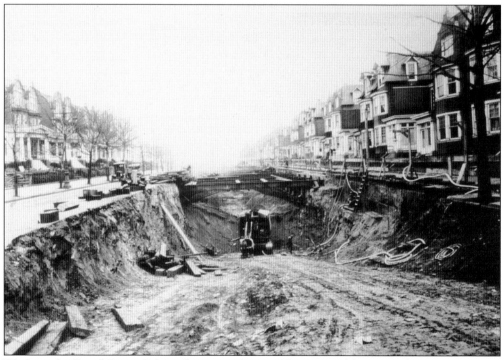

Work on the Broad Street Subway began on August 25, 1924, and by September 1, 1928, it was operational. Originally the subway stretched from Philadelphia City Hall to Olney Avenue. In 1919, state senator Samuel W. Salus attempted to redirect funds that were designated for the construction of Logan Station, but his efforts were thwarted by the Logan Improvement Association. The houses are between Duncannon and Lindley Avenues.

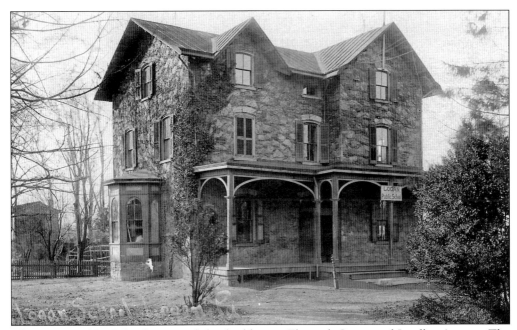

The Logan Public School occupied this building at Eleventh Street and Lindley Avenue. The small stone school has been demolished and replaced with housing. (Andrew M. Herman.)

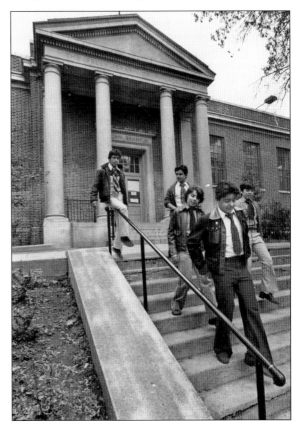

In 1903, philanthropist Andrew Carnegie donated $1.5 million to the Free Library of Philadelphia for the purpose of establishing neighborhood library branches. Through the efforts of the Logan Improvement League and Mrs. Philip Garrett, who donated the land, the Logan Branch of the Free Library of Philadelphia was built in 1917–1918. The Greek Revival–style library is located at Thirteenth Street and Wagner Avenue and continues to serve the community. (TUUA.)

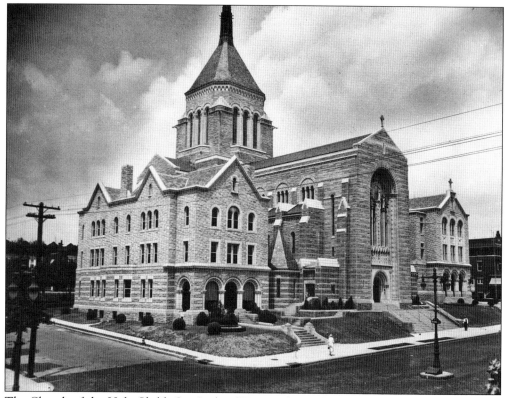

The Church of the Holy Child, Our Lady of Hope is located at the northwest corner of Broad Street and Duncannon Avenue. The first building was constructed in 1910 and was designed by E. F. Durang and Son (*fl.* 1909–1920). The large sanctuary pictured above was designed by George I. Lovatt and was completed in 1928. The Romanesque-style building features a spire, carved figures, and stained-glass windows by D'Ascenzo Studios. (TUUA.)

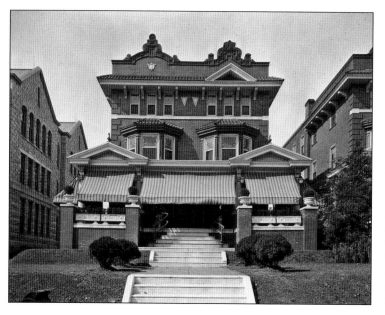

Ten elaborate twin homes were built sometime between 1910 and 1913 on the west side of Broad Street, between Fisher Street and Duncannon Avenue, just north of the Church of the Holy Child. The church purchased and converted two of the houses into a convent. They continue to serve as the church's rectory. (PhillyHistory.)

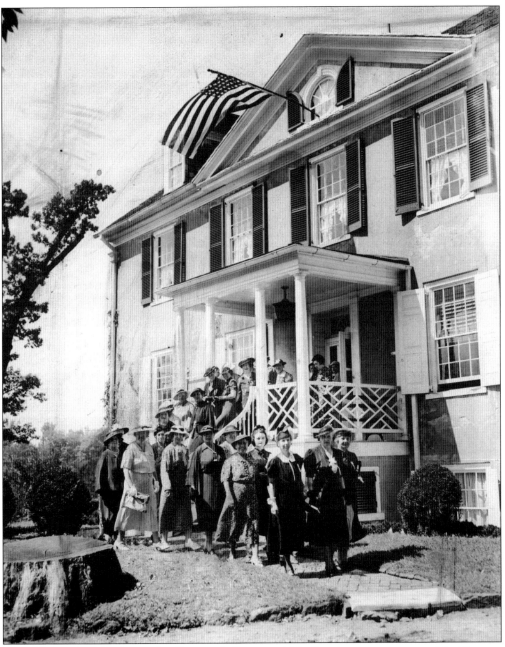

Wakefield, which was located at Sixteenth Street and Lindley Avenue, was erected by Thomas and Sarah Fisher. Sarah inherited a portion of her grandfather's estate, Stenton, and Thomas had Wakefield constructed in 1798. In 1807, Fisher's son, William Logan Fisher, purchased Roberts Mills and founded Wakefield Mills—the first knitting mill in the United States. Fisher and his descendants operated the mills, which were located near the intersection of Belfield and Lindley Avenues. The family abandoned the house and mill buildings after World War I. The Colonial Dames of America, the owners of Stenton, obtained Wakefield and used it as their headquarters from 1927 to 1957. Sadly, neither the house nor the mill buildings are extant, the house having been demolished in 1985. In 1989, La Salle University purchased the property. (FLP.)

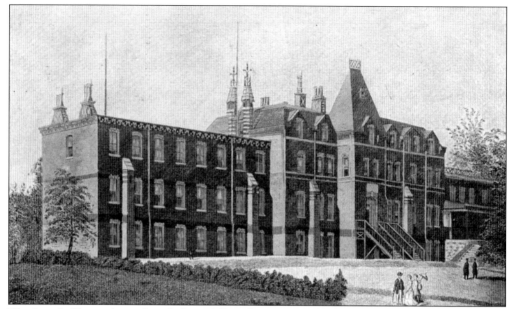

The Jewish Hospital was founded in 1865 and was originally located in West Philadelphia. In 1873, the hospital moved to a large plot at Old York Road and Olney Avenue. The hospital served the sick and wounded without regard to creed, color, or nationality. In 1952, the hospital merged with Mount Sinai Hospital and Northern Liberties Hospital to form the Albert Einstein Medical Center. (FLP.)

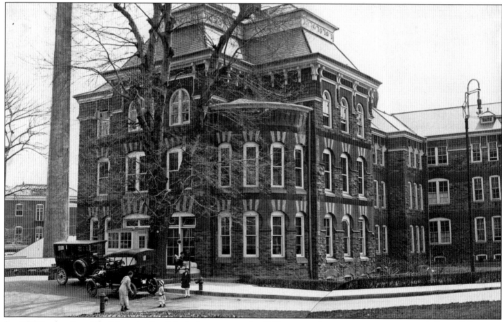

In 1903, the Jewish Hospital added three new buildings to its growing campus. The additions were the Loeb Memorial Operating Building (pictured), the Guggenheim Private Hospital, and the Eisner Home for Nurses. The Loeb Memorial Operating Building was designed by Furness, Evans, and Company (*fl.* 1886–1931). The $20,000 building was connected to the main structure via a covered bridge. It was demolished and replaced during a later expansion. (FLP.)

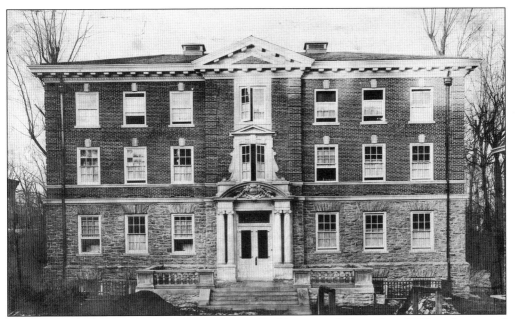

Funded largely by the state, the Pennsylvania Building was dedicated in 1908 as the nurses' home. The building was designed by the Philadelphia architectural firm Magaziner and Potter (*fl.* 1908–1917) and replaced the Eisner Building for Nurses. The Jewish Hospital Training School for Nurses opened on January 1, 1892, with Miss Douglass Benson as the school director. The school closed in 1987. (FLP.)

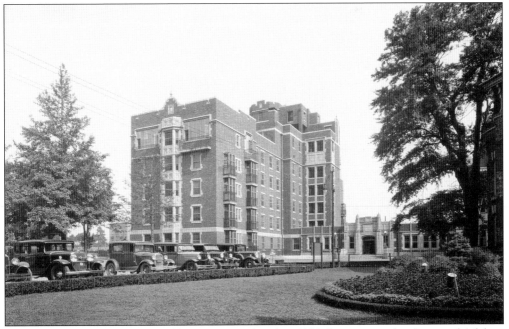

The Hackenburg Maternity Building was completed in 1928. It was named in honor of Adeline and William B. Hackenburg, who were among the founders of the hospital. The $850,000 building was designed by Philadelphia architect Horace W. Castor. It is brick with limestone and terra-cotta trim and featured a balcony on each floor and a solarium. (PhillyHistory.)

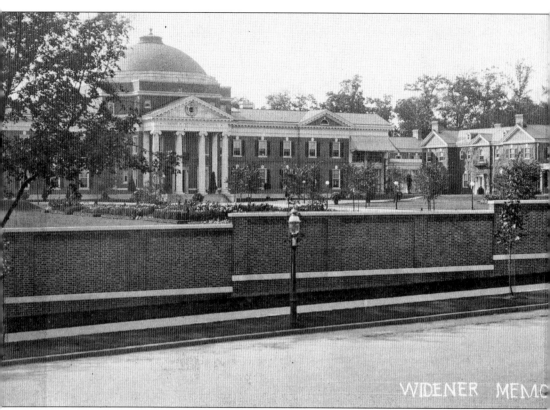

In 1899, traction magnate and philanthropist Peter A. B. Widener purchased the Charles R. Rogers estate, Beaumont, at Old York Road and Thorpe's Lane (later Olney Avenue). Shortly thereafter, Widener announced plans to build a school for crippled children in memory of his late wife, Josephine Dunton Widener, and their son Harry K. Widener. Architect Horace Trumbauer designed the school complex and builder George F. Payne and Company won the construction bid, with work commencing in the summer of 1902. On March 3, 1906, the Widener Memorial Industrial Training School for Crippled Children officially opened. The campus originally consisted of an administration building, an industrial building, a nurses' home, two cottages, a chapel, and an isolation building. The school was a combined home, medical clinic, and training school. It accepted disabled children aged 4 to 10 years who, except for occasional visits to their families, spent all of their time at the school until they came of age. The curriculum included farming, poultry raising, market gardening, watch making, and domestic service. The school was incorporated and chartered in March 1912. A month later, Widener lost his son George

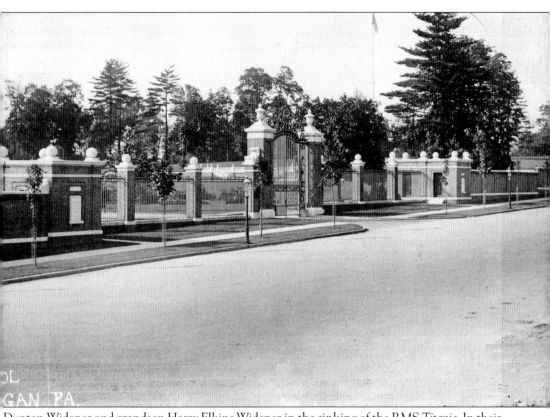

Dunton Widener and grandson Harry Elkins Widener in the sinking of the RMS *Titanic*. In their memory, Widener gave the school $4 million for its endowment. He explained, "We have taken the children from the slums and alleys. They came in half-naked and knew nothing whatever. Now they are receiving a good English education. They are being taught some business or branch of trade which their physical disabilities will not prevent following." Enrollment was limited to 125 students, although during the 1930s it dwindled, falling to 50 by 1941. Declining enrollment was due chiefly to the growing realization that handicapped children are better served medically in hospitals and educated at day schools. As a result, in 1941 the Widener School merged with the Philadelphia School District's school for handicapped children and became a day school. The old school buildings were not suited to the new operations, so they were demolished in 1950 and a new facility opened in October 1953. The brick wall and the 1904 stable building survived the overhaul. The school, which exists as the Widener Memorial School, continues to serve special needs children with a variety of cognitive and physical challenges.

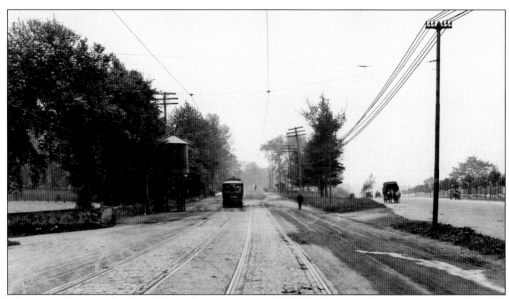

This 1911 photograph was taken at the intersection of Old York Road and Olney Avenue, looking south. At this time, Broad Street terminated at Olney Avenue. To continue north, carriages transferred to Old York Road. The road and the water tower were owned by the traction company. The water tower fed sprinklers that were used to keep the dust down on the unpaved road.

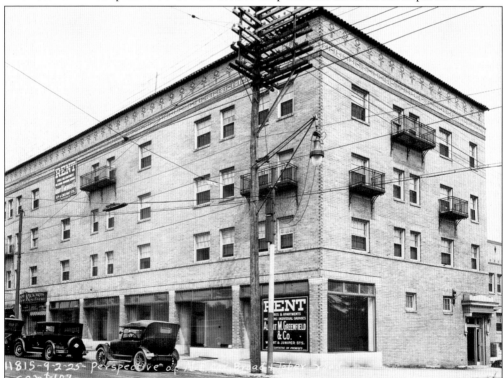

Located at the northeast corner of Old York and Tabor Roads is a commercial block that originally contained seven retail spaces. Built in the early 1920s, the building still stands, but the wide, ornate cornice has been covered and the balconies have been removed. (PhillyHistory.)

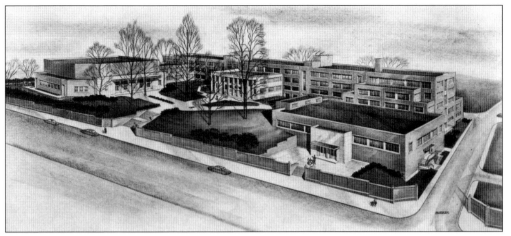

The Girls' Normal School was founded in 1848. In 1893, the school split and the Philadelphia High School for Girls became a separate entity. The normal school prepared girls for teaching and the high school prepared girls for college. In 1958, Philadelphia High School for Girls moved from Seventeenth and Spring Garden Streets into this complex at the northeast corner of Broad Street and Olney Avenue, within the original walls of the Widener School. (ATH.)

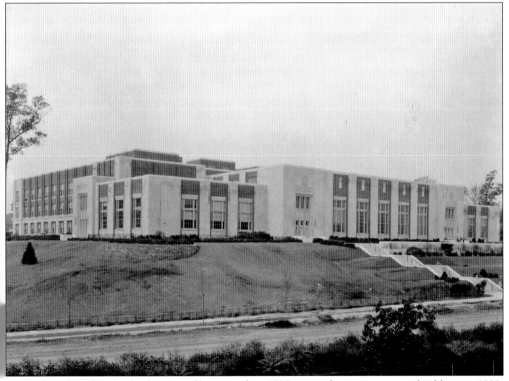

Central High School, which originally opened in 1838, moved into its present building in 1939. In 1849, the school was granted the ability to confer college degrees, the only high school in the country authorized to do this. Distinguished alumni include art collector Albert Barnes (92nd class), linguist and political activist Noam Chomsky (184th class), comedian Bill Cosby (204th class), painter Thomas Eakins (38th class), comedian Larry Fine (132nd class), and architect Louis I. Kahn (134th class). (PhillyHistory.)

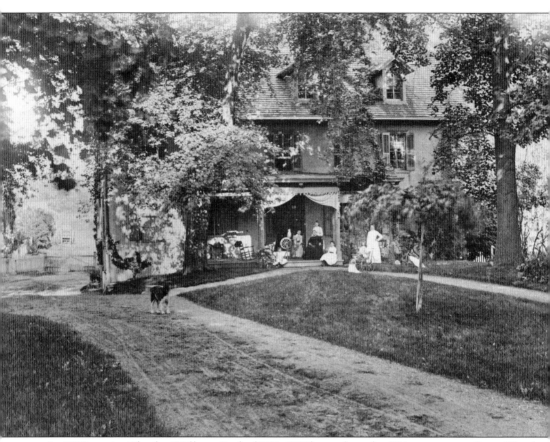

In 1810, artist Charles Willson Peale (1741–1827) purchased a 104-acre estate from Charles and Mary Gregoire. Peale named the property Belfield and promptly began improvements. He enlarged the existing house, erected outbuildings, planted an elaborate garden, and acquired farming equipment. At age 69, Peale began farming. A Maryland native, Peale studied painting under John Hesselius (1728–1778) and Benjamin West (1738–1820). He is best known for painting portraits of America's founders, including George Washington and Thomas Jefferson, and for his role in establishing the Pennsylvania Academy of Fine Arts and the Peale Museum, which was dedicated to natural history. In 1826, Peale sold the Belfield property to William Logan Fisher. The Fisher family retained ownership until 1984. Pictured in 1890 are Sarah Logan Fisher Wister and her grandchildren. In 1984, LaSalle purchased the entire estate, which included four houses, two of which, Belfield and Little Wakefield, survived. (LaSalle University.)

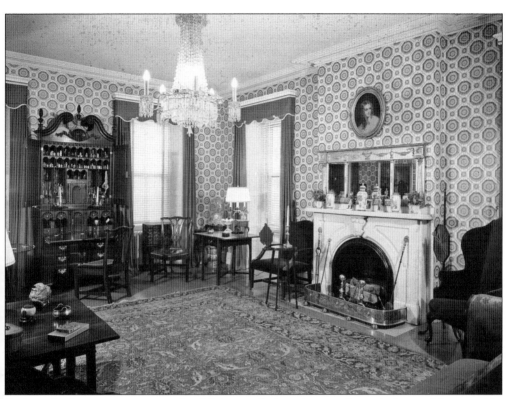

Peale and subsequent owners made additions and alterations to the main house. Most notably, Peale built a painting room on the north side of the house and reduced the number of rooms by removing interior walls. Sarah and William Logan Fisher Wister altered the roof line, connected the separate kitchen to the main house to create a laundry room, and added an elevator. Sallie and John Wister transformed the country house into a formal residence. The main parlor is now the office of LaSalle University's president. (HABS.)

Wister was built in 1876 for Sarah and William Logan Fisher's son, William Rotch Wister. The young Wister was a cricket enthusiast, and he founded the Junior Cricket Club at the University of Pennsylvania in 1842 and the Germantown Cricket Club in 1854. Wister enjoyed a successful career as a lawyer, representing the Stephen Girard Estate and the North Pennsylvania Railroad. The mansion, located near the northeast corner of Belfield Avenue and Wister Street, was demolished in 1956. (LaSalle University.)

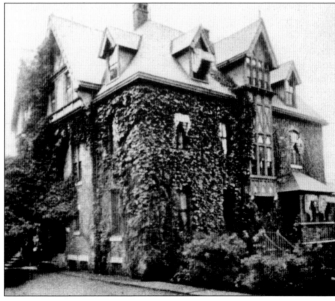

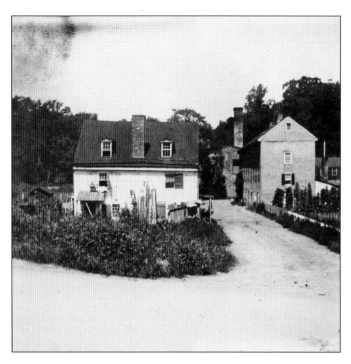

In 1807, William Logan Fisher purchased the existing Roberts Mill, which consisted of a mill with a spinning jenny and 4 acres. Roberts Mill blossomed into the Wakefield Mills Manufacturing Company, which, at its pinnacle, produced about nine-tenths of the woolen hosiery and fancy knit goods in the United States. It was located near the current intersection of Belfield and Lindley Avenues. By 1900, the mill buildings were abandoned, and after World War I, the Logan family left their adjacent estates. In 1989, LaSalle University acquired the site. No traces of the mills remain. (HSP.)

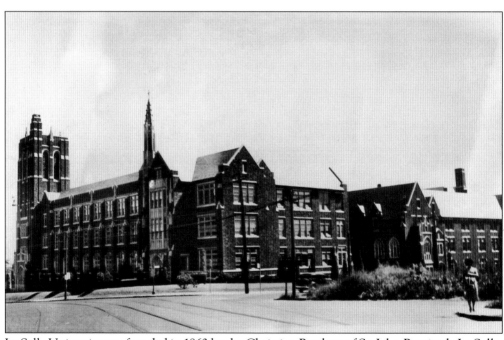

La Salle University was founded in 1863 by the Christian Brothers of St. John Baptist de La Salle. The school outgrew its quarters twice before moving to Logan. The centerpiece of the campus is the collegiate Gothic-style College Hall, which opened on February 5, 1930. College Hall, a faculty building, and a gymnasium were erected on the 11-acre site, at Twentieth Street and Olney Avenue. At that time, 110 students were enrolled and 13 instructors taught there. (ATH.)

Four

FERN ROCK

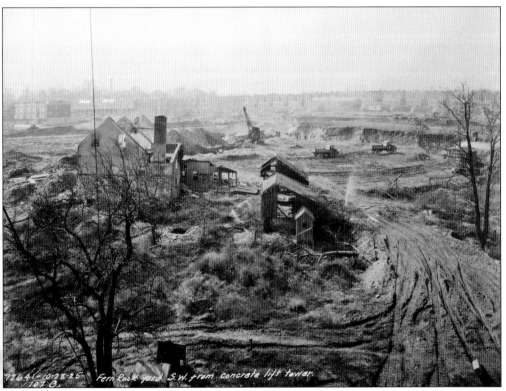

The idea for a subway line running along Broad Street dates back to the early 1900s. However, it was not until 1924 that construction began. The original line ran from Philadelphia City Hall to Olney Avenue. A train yard was required at the end of the line, so a 32-acre site bounded by Chew Street, Nedro Avenue, Marvine Street, and the Reading Railroad line was developed. Aside from a few houses, the ground was undeveloped. By October 28, 1925, the ground for the new Fern Rock Terminal Yard was being cleared and leveled. (PhillyHistory.)

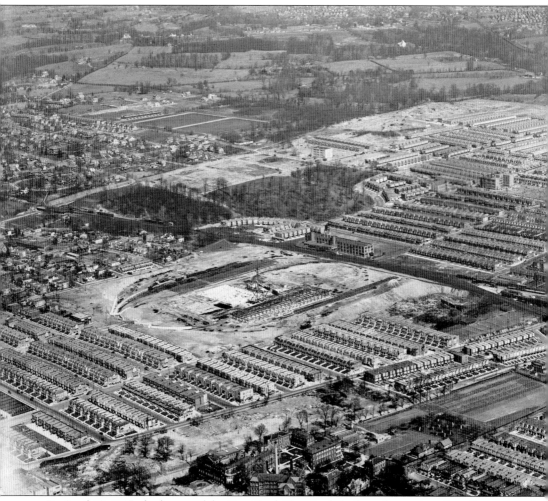

By April 13, 1927, the layout of the Fern Rock Terminal Yard was becoming clear. Storage tracks radiating from the subway tunnel entrance frame the ground upon which the service buildings begin to rise. The subway and the terminal were built by the City and operated by the Philadelphia Rapid Transit Company, a private concern. There were a number of shops within the complex that provided full servicing for the subway's fleet. The yard buildings were constructed with the surrounding residential community in mind. (TUUA.)

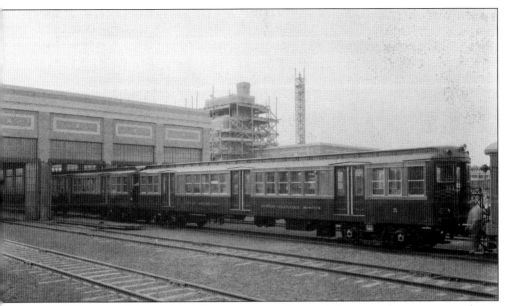

By August 1927, some of the yard buildings were complete and the new subway cars were being tested. The yard was capable of holding 165 cars, but there was ground for additional tracks so the capacity could be increased to 450 cars. The entire subway project cost $90 million and service began on September 1, 1928. The success of the line spurred its expansion south. In 1930, the line was extended to South Street, in 1932 to Snyder Avenue, and in 1973 to Pattison Avenue. (PhillyHistory.)

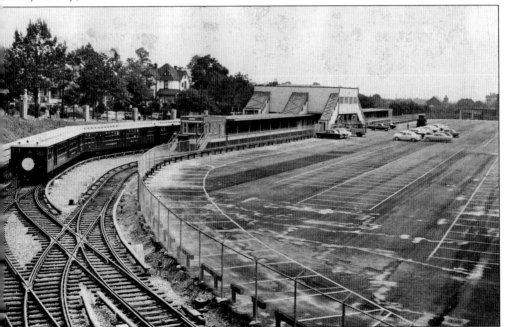

In 1956, the subway line was extended north from Olney to Fern Rock. A platform was built alongside the rail yard and trains were able to loop around the entire terminal yard complex. In May 1992, the Fern Rock Transportation Center opened, linking the subway line with the regional rail system. (TUUA.)

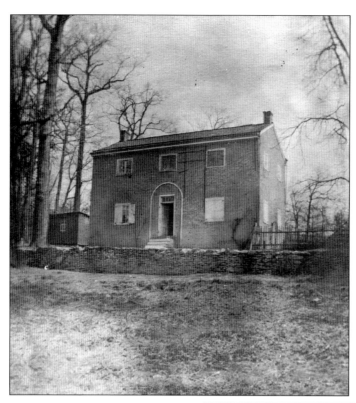

Fern Rock House was built in 1770 by Nathan Whitman. In the early 1800s, Judge John Kane (1795–1854) bought Fern Rock House and 10 acres of the Silver Pine Farm from Dr. George deBenneville Jr. Kane's property fronted onto the upper side of Green Lane. He was a politician and a lawyer who held positions as attorney general of Pennsylvania and as judge of the federal district court. His son, Dr. Elisha Kent Kane, was a famous arctic explorer. (HSP.)

Born at Fern Rock House, Dr. Elisha Kent Kane (1822–1857) graduated from the University of Pennsylvania School of Medicine and became a medical surgeon in the U.S. Navy. He was the first American hero of polar explorations, participating in two trips to the arctic. During his second expedition, the crew's fleet succumbed to ice and Kane led his men on a heroic 1,300-mile journey to safety. Kane courted Margaret Fox, one of the neighboring Fox sisters who were mediums and proponents of spirit rappings. After Kane's early death at 36, Fox styled herself Mrs. Kane, asserting that they had married. (HSP.)

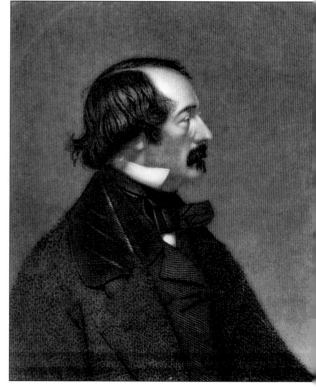

When the North Pennsylvania Railroad line began operating through the area in 1853, Fern Rock became a summer destination and the Fern Rock House was transformed into the Kenilworth Inn, a large boardinghouse and summer hotel. One of the inn's owners, a Mrs. Mather, named the inn in honor of Sir Walter Scott's famous romance novel. After returning from his second arctic expedition, Kane spent his convalescent days in 1855–1856 at the inn writing about his experiences. (PhillyHistory.)

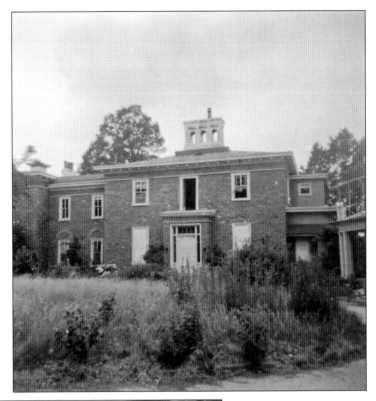

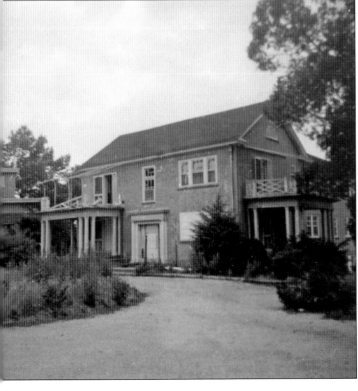

Thomas Leiper Kane (1822–1883), the other son of Judge John Kane, was a staunch abolitionist. While he and his wife lived with Judge Kane at Fern Rock House, they assisted fleeing slaves, making the location a stop on the Underground Railroad. Judge Kane enforced the Federal Slavery Laws in court but colluded with his son's antislavery actions at home. The Kenilworth Inn stood at the corner of Tenth Street and Godfrey Avenue for more than 100 years and was demolished around 1964 to make way for apartments. (PhillyHistory.)

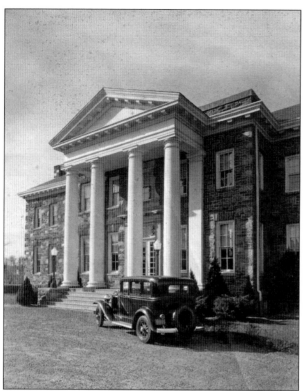

The Pennsylvania State College of Optometry opened at 1809 Spring Garden Street in 1919. In 1932, college president Dr. Albert Fitch learned of the availability of a complex of buildings facing Godfrey Avenue that had served as the Home for Hebrew Orphans. The college purchased the 7-acre property and relocated to the site. The old main building was used for classroom and laboratory space. Many students found dormitory rooms in local homes. (Salus University.)

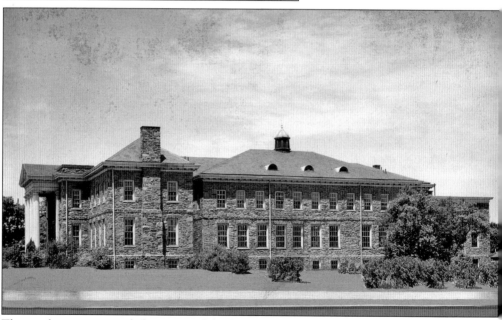

The purchase, repair, and alterations of the former orphanage cost $125,000. The renovation of the grounds through landscaping brought out the natural beauty of the location. The college purchased adjacent lots over the years, increasing the campus to 20 acres. The college retained its Spring Garden location, though remodeled in order to better teach clinical skills. (Salus University.)

Students formally dressed in vests and ties ran their experiments in a chemistry laboratory class given by Dr. Jacob Nevyas. The college admitted women to its program early on. Curriculum requirements for graduation became increasingly strict, and by 1935 the course was four years in length. Dr. Albert Fitch was held in such high regard that his four-year time period for graduation soon became the standard for optometry colleges across the nation. (Salus University.)

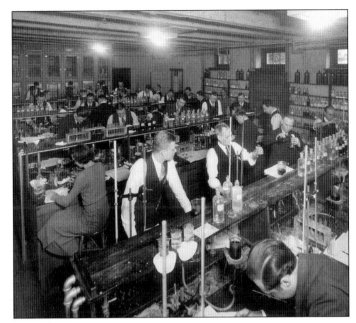

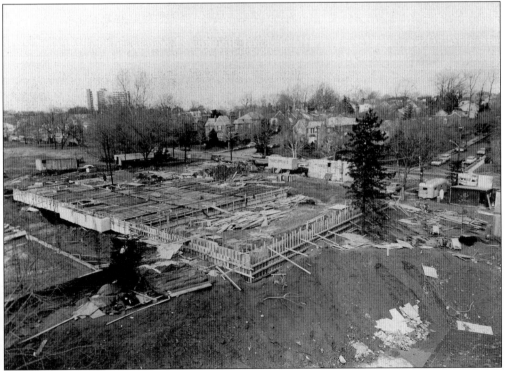

Dr. Lawrence Fitch headed the college for 12 years after his father's death in 1960. He oversaw the demolition of the old main building and the construction of more modern structures on the site. In 1964, the college was renamed the Pennsylvania College of Optometry. The state-of-the-art Eye Institute was built in 1978. In 1998, the college moved to Elkins Park; however, it still maintains the Eye Institute at Fern Rock. In 2008, the college established Salus University and became one of the university's four colleges. (Salus University.)

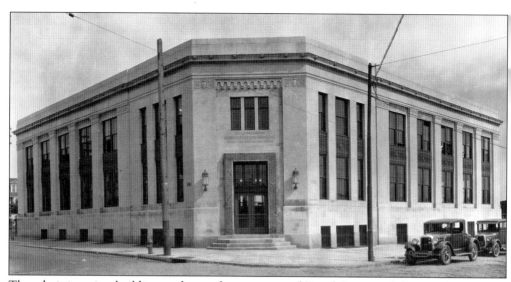

The administration building at the southeast corner of Broad Street and Grange Avenue was headquarters of the Broad Street Subway's trainmen and operating staff. It was deceptively large, composed of five stories—two-and-a-half of which were below ground—directly above the subway. The administrative and operating staffs were housed in the floors aboveground, and the office of the receiver was in the basement. The aboveground stories were removed in 2009. (TUUA.)

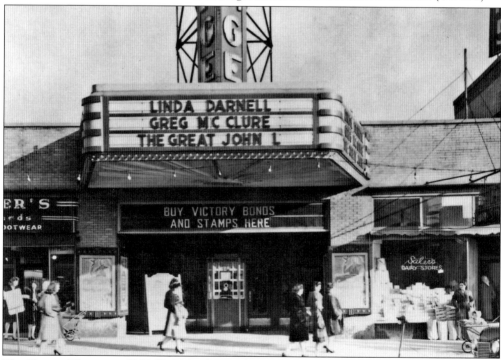

The Grange Theater at 5717–5719 North Broad Street was a popular venue that premiered films and had a seating capacity of 1,000. In this photograph, the marquee advertises *The Great John L* (1945), a popular screen biography of the famous boxer John L. Sullivan. William Goldman Theaters took over the Grange from Warner Brothers, extensively renovated it, and reopened it as the Esquire Theater. It closed in late 1970s. (ATH.)

Five

WEST OAK LANE

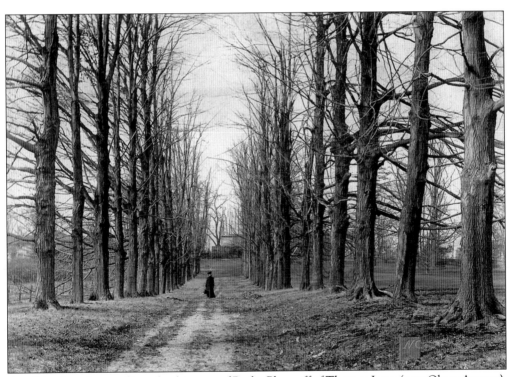

An allée of maple trees lines the driveway of Butler Place off of Thorpes Lane (now Olney Avenue). The estate was bordered by Church Lane, Old York Road, Thorpes Lane, and Mill Creek. The main house on the estate was built by French merchant Frederick Boulanger in 1791. Pierce Butler, a former officer in the British army and later a delegate from South Carolina to the Constitutional Convention, purchased the property in 1810 and adjoining land in 1812.

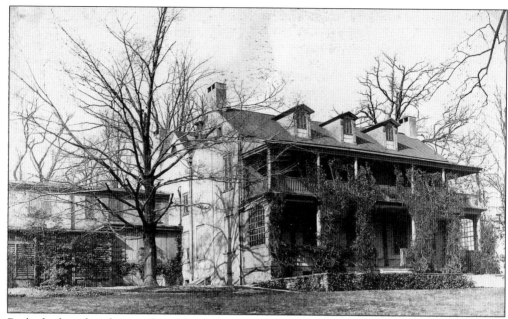

Butler had made a fortune from his plantations along the sea islands of Georgia and had lived in Philadelphia since the 1790s. His daughter and son-in-law, Sarah and James Mease, had three sons. Butler, having no male descendants to inherit his plantation fortune, offered his grandsons his entire estate should they take the Butler surname as their own. All three boys would, including the newly renamed Pierce Butler Jr.

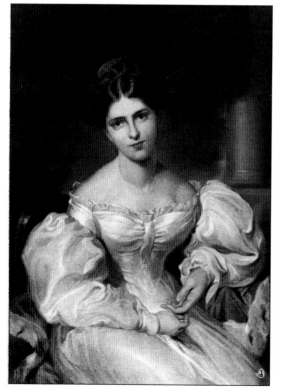

Frances Anne "Fanny" Kemble (1809–1893), was born in England into an acting family. She came to America in 1832 and soon became the most popular young actress of the day. In 1834, she married Pierce Butler Jr. and they had two daughters, Sarah and Frances. In 1838, Butler took his wife to his plantation in Georgia, where she was appalled at the institution of slavery. The couple had a rocky marriage almost from the start and they divorced in 1849. In 1877, Kemble left for England, never to return. Butler, meanwhile, squandered two fortunes and remained under watch as a Southern sympathizer throughout the Civil War. He died in 1867. (HSP.)

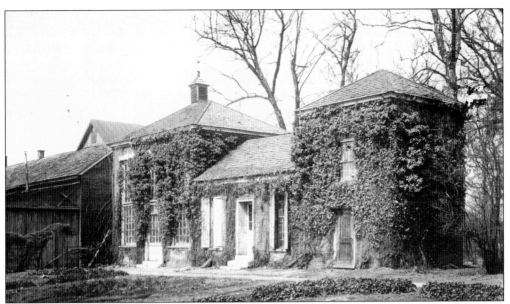

Butler Place had extensive gardens, a number of out buildings, and a double piazza that extended from the lower side of the main house. The detached English-style walled garden included fig and other semitropical trees. After the death of Pierce Butler Jr., Butler Place passed to his daughter Sarah, who married Dr. Owen Jones Wister. Their son, Owen Wister (1860–1938), became a writer of western novels including *The Viriginian* (1902). Wister sold Butler Place sometime after 1922 to the Fern Rock Building Association, and the property was cleared in 1925. (FLP.)

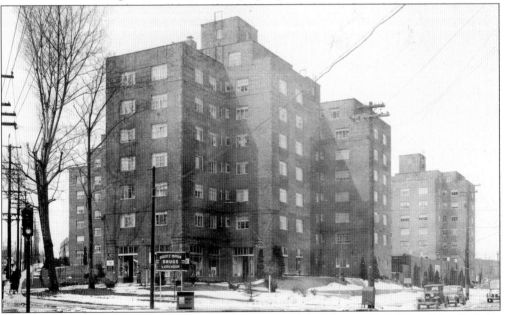

Architect George S. Idell (1886–1971) designed a set of three towers in 1939–1940 called the Ogontz Manor Apartment Houses located at 5600 North Ogontz Avenue at Olney Avenue. Ogontz Manor was in operation for over 59 years until 1996 when the city condemned the 208-unit complex. After a renovation, LaSalle University began renting the buildings for students. After another makeover, it is now open as the Julian Apartments. (FLP.)

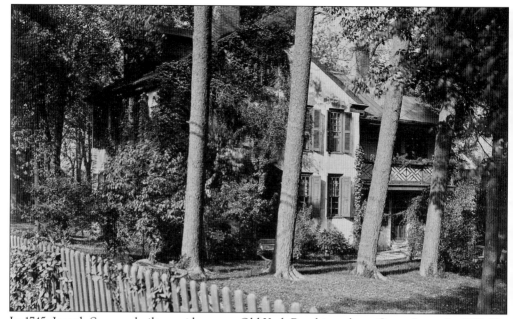

In 1745, Joseph Spencer built a residence on Old York Road just above Green Lane. In 1758, Dr. George deBenneville acquired the home. DeBenneville came to America in 1741 and settled in Oley, near Reading, before moving to Philadelphia in 1755. DeBenneville was the first physician in the area and was a preacher who founded the Universalist Church in America. His son, Dr. Daniel deBenneville, named the property Silver Pine Farm because of the numerous white pines.

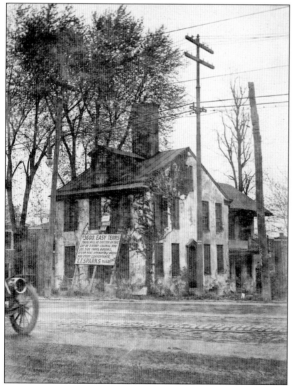

After the death of Dr. Daniel deBenneville in the mid-1800s, the house was rented out, first to local farmers, then in 1904, to the Forty-Second Ward Republican Club. In 1909, the family sold the 13-acre property to developers who demolished the home. The sign reads, "There will be erected on this lot 50 2 story Colonial houses side yards and rooms steam heat springfed water and every convenience."

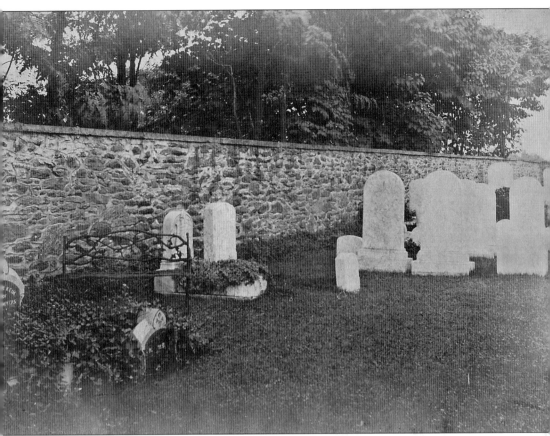

As part of his original estate, Dr. George deBenneville set aside land for a private family burial ground. The deBenneville Burial Ground at Green Lane and Old York Road is one of the oldest private cemeteries in Philadelphia. In addition to many generations of the family, the cemetery holds the remains of two senior British officers, Brig. Gen. James Tanner Agnew and Lt. Col. John Bird, who were killed during the Battle of Germantown on October 4, 1777. When the British withdrew from Philadelphia in the spring of 1778, they feared that the graves of these two officers would be desecrated and so deBenneville offered to provide space for them in his family burial ground. In 1862, Benneville D. Brown enclosed the eastern portion of the cemetery, and in 1874 his sister enclosed the western grounds. In 1902, the city took part of the eastern portion of the cemetery at a much lower grade for Broad Street. This required that 17 remains (including the British officers) be moved to another part of the graveyard. The cemetery land along Old York Road was sold to support the cemetery from which funds continue to provide for a caretaker.

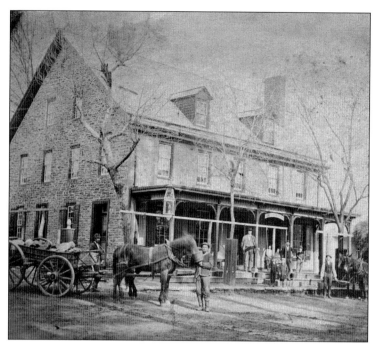

The Branchtown Hotel was built around 1790 by Joseph Spenser. The hotel was located on Old York Road and served the many wagon drivers and stagecoaches that passed by. The Limekiln Turnpike passed through the original property. For a time, the hotel was the polling station for the surrounding district and served as the post office. On the grounds where the old hotel once stood now stands Christ Baptist Church, established in 1955.

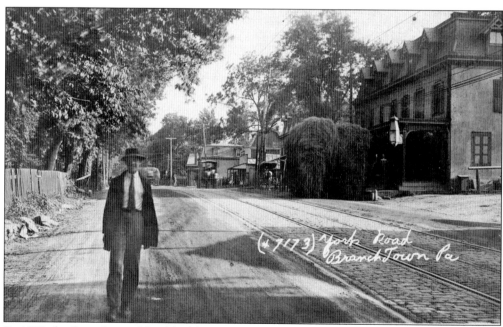

By 1897, the Branchtown Hotel had been expanded to include a full third level complete with a mansard roof. In the late 1800s, the hotel was owned by Hamilton Clayton, and during his proprietorship, the hotel became famous as a resort for sleighing parties. Clayton sold the hotel to Davis N. Hallowell in 1903. Throughout the first half of the 20th century, the hotel was able to continue and it served as a popular stop for funeral parties returning from Northwood Cemetery.

Jacob Rorer's general country store, as seen in 1882 after a fire, was situated on the southeast corner of Old York Road and Green Lane. When this fire occurred, Jacob Rorer and his son lost $30,000. Rorer bought the land and stone building from Jacob Miller, whose son, Daniel H. Miller, was a member of Congress. In 1853, Rorer helped organize the Germantown and Branchtown Turnpike and Plank Road Company. After the fire, a Mr. Mingin acquired the store and modernized it.

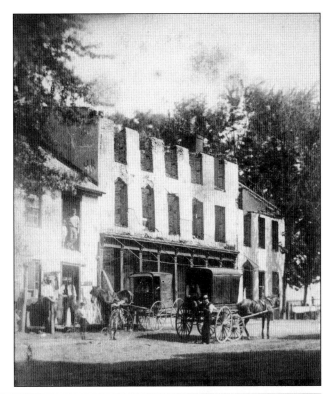

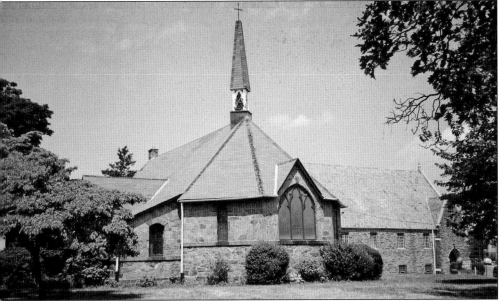

The House of Prayer of the Protestant Episcopal Church at 1725 Church Lane was built in 1862 on land donated by Anne deBenneville Mears. The architect, Emlen Littell (1838–1891), used an early English Gothic design for the chapel. Other buildings on the grounds include the parish house, first erected in 1875 and replaced in 1925, as well as a parish rectory built in 1908. A memorial with a bronze bas relief that was donated by Clement Biddle Barclay stands on the high ground above the Church Lane wall. (Marita Krivda.)

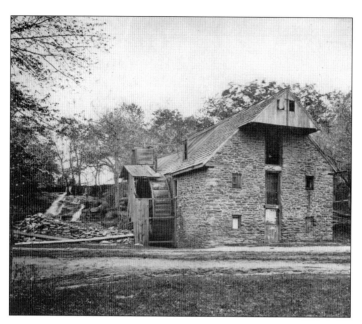

In 1683, Richard Townsend established the Townsend Mill on the north side of Mill Street (now Church Lane), about a mile from Germantown at the point where the street crossed Mill Creek, a tributary of the Wingohocking Creek. An English millwright, Townsend arrived in Philadelphia the preceding year with William Penn. His was the third gristmill in the Philadelphia region. Later the mill was sold to the Lukens family and was called Lukens Mill in the 1770s. (FLP.)

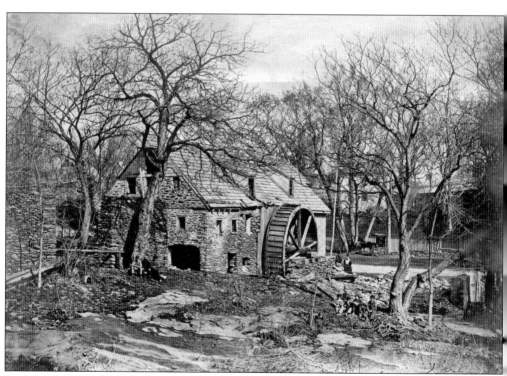

In the early 1800s, Hugh Roberts acquired the mill, and it became know as the Roberts Mill. The mill closed in 1858 and was demolished in 1874. In the decade after the mill closed, city engineers drew up drainage plans for all 129 square miles of Philadelphia. Their plans relied heavily on using existing small streams as combined storm and sewage drains. In the 1880s, the City began covering the Wingohocking Creek and its tributaries as part of this effort. (FLP.)

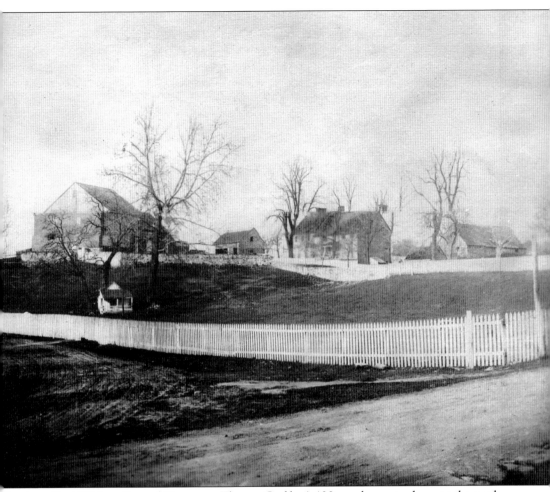

Purchased in 1697 from Samuel Carpenter, Thomas Godfrey's 100-acre homestead was on the south side of Mill Street opposite the Roberts home and near the site of the Roberts Mill. The second Thomas Godfrey, grandson of his namesake, invented the quadrant, a device for determining longitude that was put to practical use by Joshua Fisher to accurately measure Cape Henlopen. Thomas Godfrey III lived on the homestead and was a playwright who penned *Prince of Parthia* (1765), the first American play to be performed by a professional cast of actors. During the 1830s, John Button lived in the Godfrey home and carried on the manufacturing of hosiery using his own needles made with imported English wire. His grandson, Conyers Button (1839–1924), built the Conyers Button Germantown Hosiery Mills in 1886 on East Walnut Lane and Hancock Street. (GHS.)

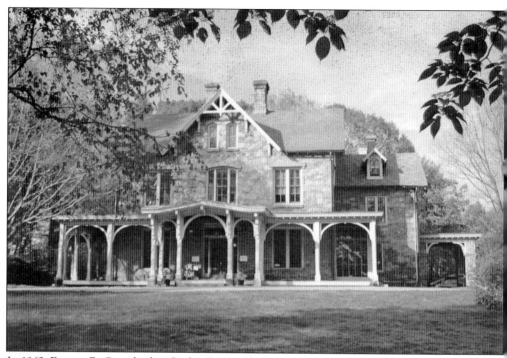

In 1862, Francis R. Cope built a Gothic Revival home on 40 acres of land his father had purchased in 1852. Cope was the grandson of Thomas Pym Cope, the Quaker founder of the famous Cope packet ships that sailed from Philadelphia to Liverpool. The name of the estate, Awbury, was derived from the family's ancestral home in England. Succeeding generations of the Cope family lived on the property. Since 2001, fifty-five acres with 24 historic buildings have been known as the Awbury Historic District. (AAA.)

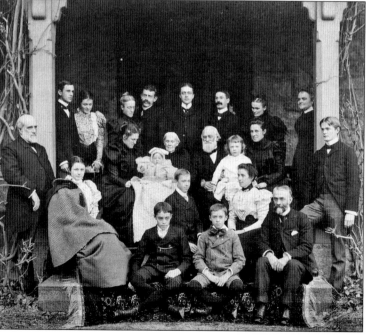

Francis Reeve Cope and Anna Stewardson Brown Cope celebrated their 50th wedding anniversary at Awbury on December 16, 1897, surrounded by their family. Awbury's extended family property began with the contiguous country estates of John Haines, Thomas P. Cope, and Francis R. Cope. Great trees dominated the early landscape; William Saunders and Thomas P. Cope were the chief landscape designers. (AAA.)

The John Smith Haines Wisteria Arbor was built to add dramatic interest to his gardens. In addition to this arbor, another long arbor near the Thomas P. Cope House was covered with grapevine and trumpet vine. It was built to give the children a shady place to play. A later Victorian garden had old-fashioned roses, peonies, hollyhocks, and snapdragons. Greenhouses attested to an abiding interest in horticulture. (AAA.)

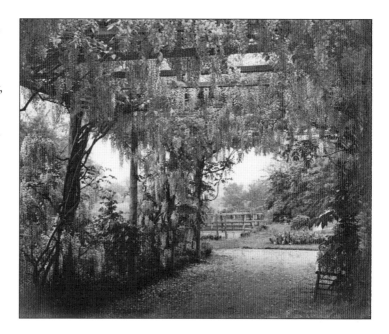

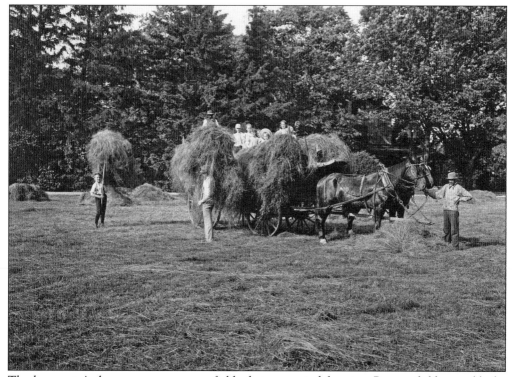

The lawns at Awbury were once open fields that supported farming. Pasture fields, a stable for horses, and sheds for cows were shared. The hay fields had moveable iron fence panels made in England to keep farm animals from straying. The open land was turned over to the City Parks Association in 1917 to preserve the green space and avoid subdivisions. Twenty-four houses on the property were kept in private hands. (AAA.)

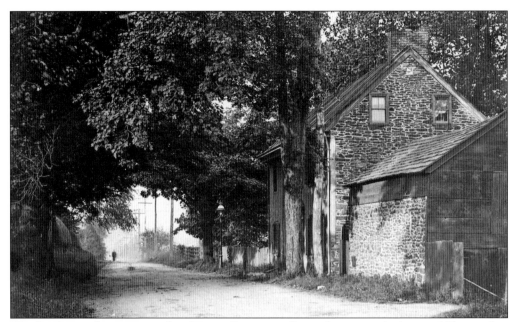

The farmhouse that once stood on Haines Street near Boyer Street was the home of Christopher Ludwick (1720–1801). Ludwick was a German immigrant who prospered in Philadelphia, first as a gingerbread baker and later as the "Baker-General" of the Continental army. His 33-acre farm was later owned by John Haines. Ludwick set up a charitable foundation at his death, which continues to this day providing education grants to poor children. (AAA.)

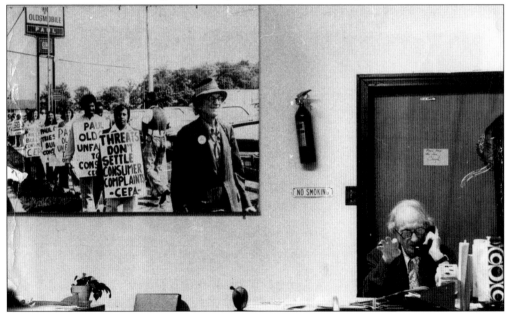

Max Weiner, busy at work in his office at 6048 Ogontz Avenue in 1980, founded the Consumer Education and Protection Association (CEPA) in 1970 to rectify unjust real estate and automobile sales transactions. The consumer advocate extraordinaire resided in East Oak Lane with his wife, Besse. Their home was at 6416 North Eighth Street. CEPA still remains one of Philadelphia's leading consumer advocacy organizations. (TUUA.)

The architectural firms of Hoffman-Henon Company and Magaziner, Eberhard, and Harris (*fl.* 1922–1930) designed the Ogontz Theatre at 6033-6043 Ogontz Avenue in 1926. The exterior facade contained Moorish arches, columns, and half-domed windows. The Ogontz had a seating capacity of 1,777. It closed in 1988 and was demolished shortly thereafter. The Free Library built the David Cohen Branch Library on the lot adjacent to the old theater. (ATH.)

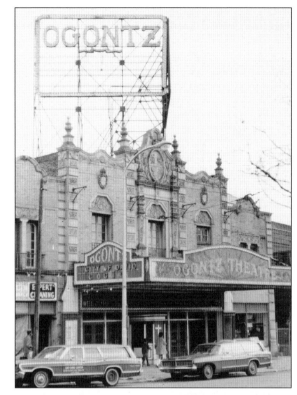

The interior of the Ogontz Theatre was lavishly decorated in a baroque style. Complete with a velvet draped proscenium arch, the theater was used for live stage performances and movie screenings well into the 1960s. The Ogontz Avenue Revitalization Corporation has been bringing live performances to Ogontz Avenue every June since 2003 with the West Oak Lane Jazz Festival. (ATH.)

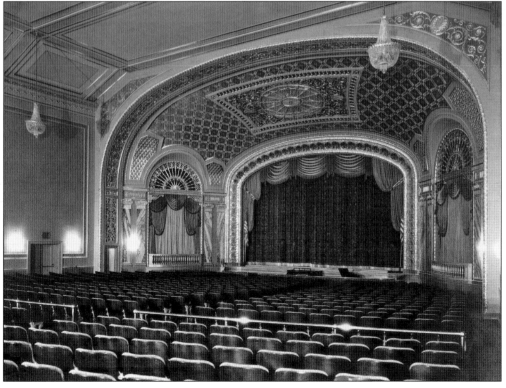

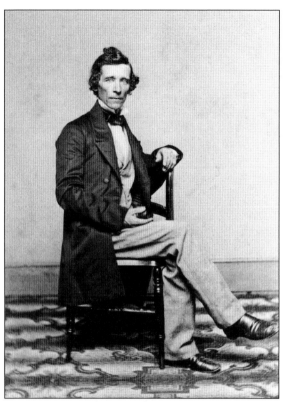

Artist Russell Smith (1812–1896) studied art in Pittsburgh during his youth with James Reid Lambdin (1807–1889). He painted the scenery for a local theatrical group, where his talents caught the eye of touring theater impresario Francis Courtney Wemyss. Wemyss hired Smith and brought him to Philadelphia in 1835. Smith was so successful in painting curtains for theaters all along the East Coast that he gave up his theater work to become a landscape painter in 1840. In 1856, Smith was persuaded to return to the theater world to paint the drop curtain for the new Academy of Music. Smith would remain the Academy's principal scenic painter until he retired in 1881. He continued to paint and exhibit landscapes throughout his life. His wife, Mary (1819–1874), and their children, Xanthus (1839–1929) and Mary (1842–1878), were also accomplished artists.

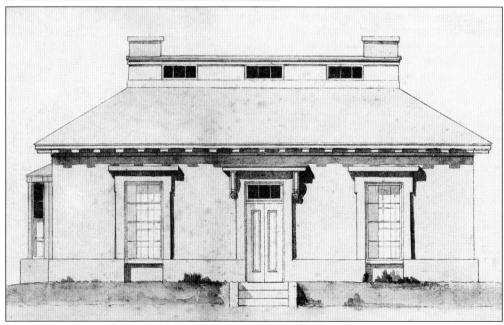

In 1840, Smith purchased land at Old York Road and Chelten Avenue. He designed a home, named Rockhill, and his family lived here until the Consolidation Act of 1854. After that, Smith wanted no part of the city and sold his estate to Joseph Wharton, who removed the Smith house. Smith purchased property in Glenside and built a new home, Edge Hill, which still stands.

Joseph Wharton was the fifth child of 10 in a wealthy Hicksite Quaker family. His early business acumen led him to excel in the manufacture of metals. He joined the Pennsylvania and Lehigh Zinc Company near Bethlehem, Pennsylvania. He was a good manager and soon took over control of the company. Later he acquired a controlling interest in the Bethlehem Steel Company. His philanthropy included a $100,000 gift that started the Wharton School at the University of Pennsylvania.

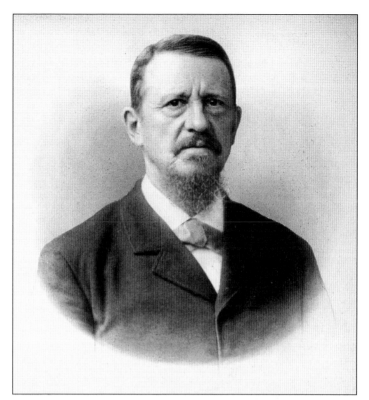

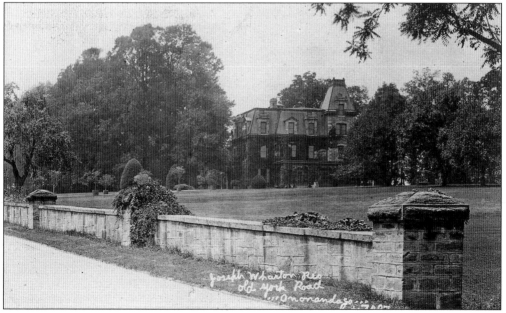

Ontalauna was the 63-acre estate of Joseph Wharton on Old York Road, north of Chelten Avenue. Ontalauna was a Native American word meaning "Little Branch." The family moved into the sandstone French Second Empire–style mansion in 1881. On the ground where Ontalauna was built was the cave of Benjamin Lay (1681–1750), an eccentric Quaker and early opponent of human slavery.

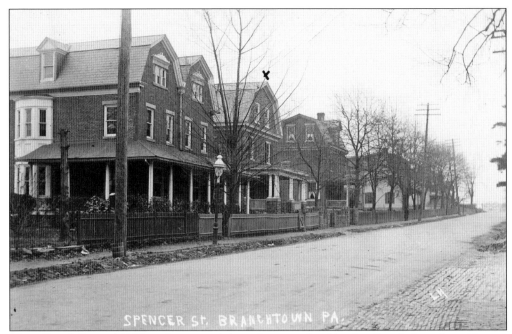

Three Dutch Revival 1900-era homes with large front porches blend well with the colonial homes further east on Spencer Street. Owners of these homes in 1923 included Max Seeger, John Scheck, Frank Romeg, and Robert M. Pollock. Old names for this area included Goat Hill and, to its west, Fenian Hill, which was named after a legendary ghost cat.

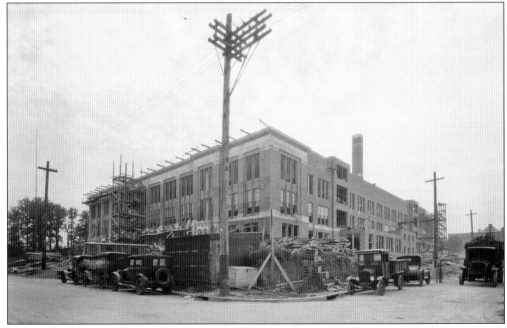

General Louis Wagner Middle School, located at 1701 West Chelten Avenue, was named after the commander of Camp William Penn—the largest Union training camp for African American troops. In 1927, architect Irwin Thornton Catharine designed the school in the classical revival style using brick, concrete, and steel. (PhillyHistory.)

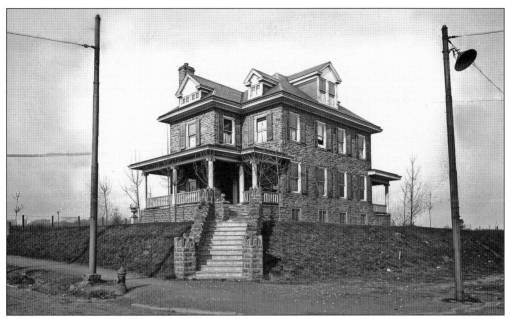

The trolley line to Willow Grove Park through Glenside ran in front of the Raffeto house. South Philadelphia carpenter Louis Raffeto purchased the corner house in 1907. The house was situated on a large estate that once held a mansion owned by Joseph Paul and his children. A realtor in 1925 began calling this area West Oak Lane to distinguish it from Oak Lane, which was east of Broad Street. (PhillyHistory.)

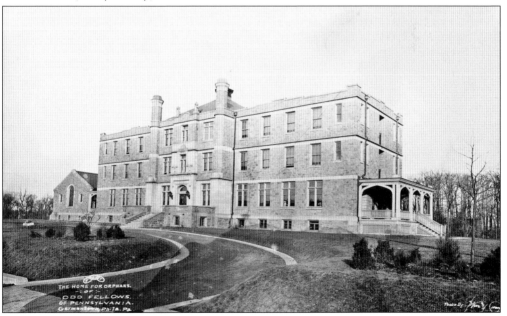

In 1907, James D. Thompson bequeathed money for the construction of an orphanage to the Odd Fellows. In 1910, the architectural firm of Furness, Evans and Company designed the Home for Orphans of the Odd Fellows of Pennsylvania at the intersection of Chelten Avenue and the newly laid out Ogontz Avenue. The building was sold in 1966 to the Mount Airy Church of God with a covenant preventing its demolition. (Odd Fellows.)

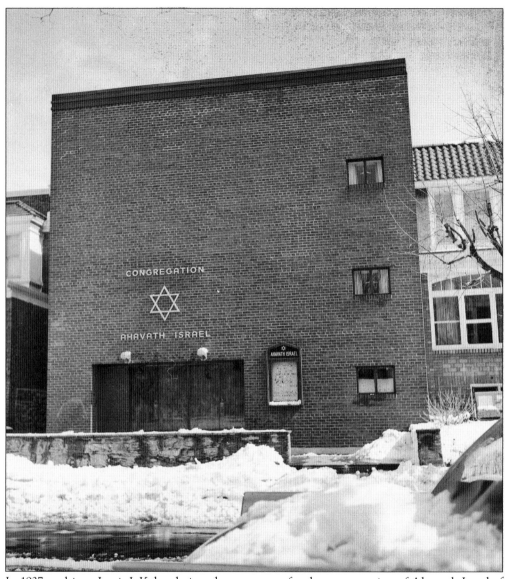

In 1937, architect Louis I. Kahn designed a synagogue for the congregation of Ahavath Israel of West Oak Lane. The modest, urban structure was built for a congregation comprised predominantly of Eastern European immigrants. The synagogue was located at 6735–6737 North Sixteenth Street in the middle of a row of ordinary brick homes. When Ahavath Israel closed in 1982, it sold the synagogue to Gratz College for $1. Kahn was professor of architecture at the University of Pennsylvania from 1957 until his death in 1974. He became something of a philosopher-in-residence at the university. His humanistic values were the foundation for his bold use of elemental geometric designs, and his buildings were landmark statements that perpetuated Philadelphia's leadership in architecture's modernism movement. Kahn's most famous works include the Kimbell Art Museum in Fort Worth, Texas; the Salk Institute in La Jolla, California; the Richards Laboratories at the University of Pennsylvania; and the National Assembly Building in Dhaka, Bangladesh. (UPPA.)

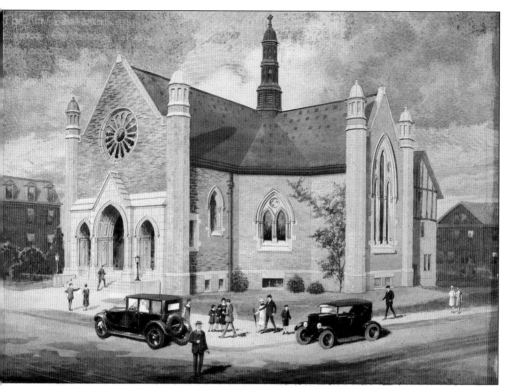

The congregation of St. Mark's Evangelical Lutheran Church was formed in 1850, and their first church was located in Center City. When that congregation merged with the Church of the Holy Spirit in 1920, the building was too small to accommodate the number of churchgoers. A new sanctuary was designed by church architects John J. Dull (1859–1949) and Norman Hulme (1887–1964) and was dedicated on December 13, 1925. The congregation continues today in this Gothic church at the corner of Broad Street and Chelten Avenue. (LTS.)

Architect John T. Windrim (1866–1934) designed the Bell Telephone building at 5469 Old York Road in 1924 in the Georgian style. Windrim was the son of Philadelphia architect James H. Windrim (1840–1919), and he took over his father's highly lucrative practice. Windrim designed more than 60 Bell Telephone buildings, as well as 30 buildings for the Philadelphia Electric Company.

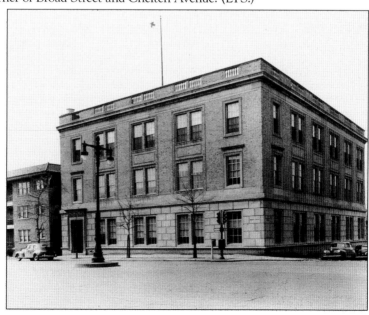

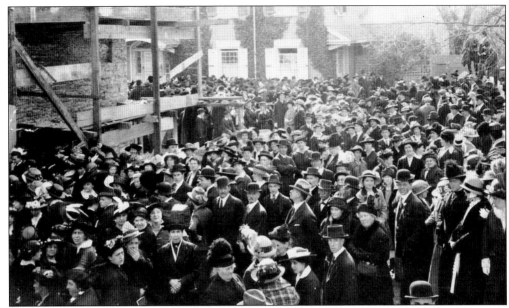

On September 26, 1915, a crowd of 10,000 people gathered for the dedication of the finished portion of the Carmelite Monastery Chapel at the corner of Old York Road and what would become Sixty-sixth Avenue. In 1902, the Discalced Carmelite Order came to Philadelphia, and in 1910 the order's founder, Mother Beatrix (Camilla Josephine Magers), purchased Hill Top, a 3.5-acre estate, from William Morris Davis. (DCO.)

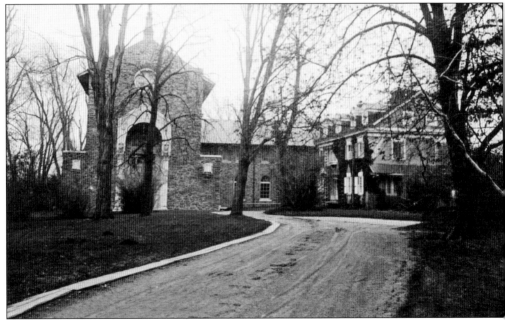

The Discalced Carmelite Order hired Maginnis and Walsh (*fl.* 1908–1955) of Boston to design their monastery. Considered Italian Byzantine, the monastery was constructed with local stone, white terra-cotta, Spanish roof tiles, and interior gray brick. The monastery contains an interior cloister walk, a turn room, an enclosed central courtyard, and a wing for living quarters. D'Ascenzo Studios designed the exceptional stained glass in the chapel. (DCO.)

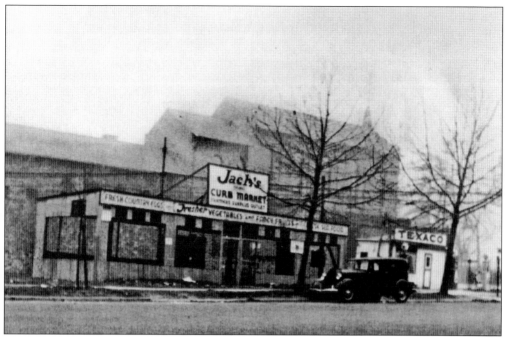

Jack's Curb Market was located at the corner of Broad Street and Sixty-sixth Avenue around 1928. Texaco was the first U.S. oil company to sell its gasoline nationwide under its own brand name. This location is the current site of the Oak Lane Diner, which started in the mid-1930s following the demolition of the market and gas station. Wray Wiley bought the stainless steel diner in 1944 and redesigned it using Paramount silver glazing balls on the rounded corners. (DCO.)

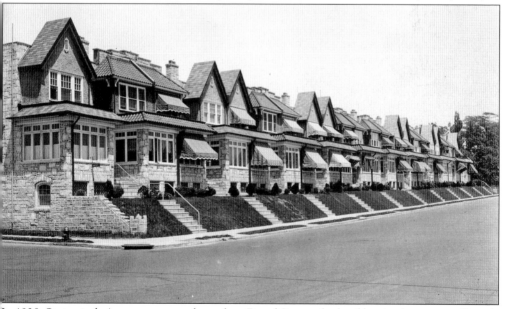

In 1928, Sixty-sixth Avenue was put through to Broad Street, the land having been part of Joseph Wharton's extensive land holdings. The houses on the north side of the road in the 1500 block were built within the year and were quickly purchased. Street trees were later planted. All of the houses still stand today.

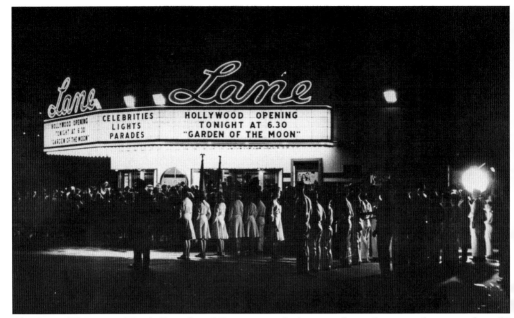

The Lane Theater at North Broad and Sixty-seventh Avenue showed movies for more than 50 years. William Freihofer, a wealthy investor in movie houses, built an earlier theater on this site in 1927 at the staggering cost of $500,000. This first moving-picture house had a stage for vaudeville acts. In 1938, the theater was redesigned just for movies. It held a Hollywood-style reopening that featured the musical comedy *Garden of the Moon* (1938) on October 1, 1938. (ATH.)

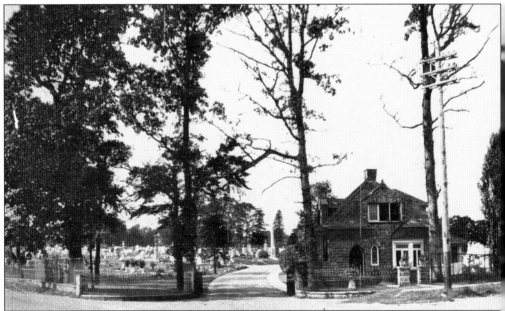

The Northwood Cemetery Company, founded in 1878, purchased 101 acres between Haines Street and the City Line (Cheltenham Avenue) with a front connecting entrance to Old York Road. Noteworthy burials within include legendary baseball star Kid Gleason (1866–1933), sacred music composer Joseph Lincoln Hall (1866–1930), and the original soul sister of gospel music, Sister Rosetta Tharpe (1915–1973). (GHS.)

The National Cemetery was established in 1862 and is located at Limekiln Pike and Haines Street. It sits on 15 acres of federally owned land and contains the remains of more than 10,000 veterans, 2,700 of whom were Civil War Union soldiers. In 1927, the remains of 169 soldiers who fought in the Mexican-American War were removed from Glenwood Cemetery and reburied at the National Cemetery. The old Mexican War Monument was removed and placed near the entrance. (Marita Krivda.)

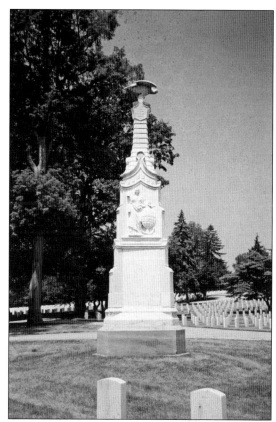

One of the villages that used to exist within the West Oak Lane area was Pittville, named after William Pitt, a local landowner. These Pittville houses faced Grant Street, a private lane on Haines Street, very near Limekiln Pike. When the farmhouses were torn down in 1936, the William Rowen School was built. William Rowen had been the president of the Board of Public Education in Philadelphia from 1921 to 1933. (PhillyHistory.)

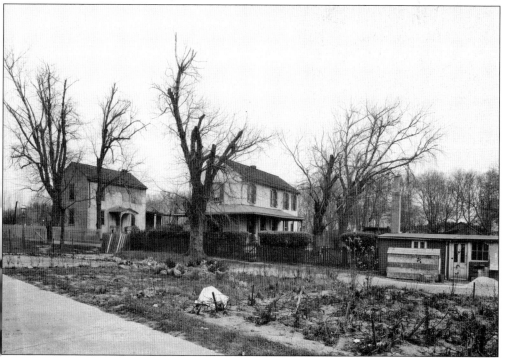

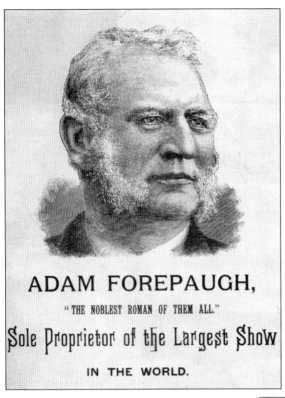

ADAM FOREPAUGH,

"THE NOBLEST ROMAN OF THEM ALL."

Sole Proprietor of the Largest Show

IN THE WORLD.

Another early village in West Oak Lane was Somerville, home to Adam Forepaugh (1831–1890), owner of the Adam Forepaugh Circus and chief rival of the P. T. Barnum Circus. Forepaugh owned land bordered by Stenton Avenue, Medary, and Twentieth Street, which he used as part of the winter quarters for his circus. (Circus World.)

When Forepaugh entered the circus world, he was independently wealthy from his days in the horse dealing business. Through the 1870s and into the 1880s, Forepaugh and P. T. Barnum had the two largest circuses in the nation, and the two constantly fought each other in the press. Forepaugh actually had more animals than Barnum and had the famous elephant, Bolivar. Bolivar was promoted as the largest living elephant, standing 10 feet in height at the shoulder. Forepaugh gave the elephant to the Philadelphia Zoo on Christmas Day 1888, where the giant pachyderm resided until his death in 1908. (FLP.)

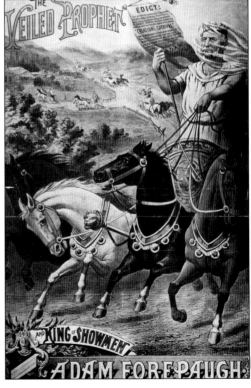

INDEX

www.arcadiapublishing.com

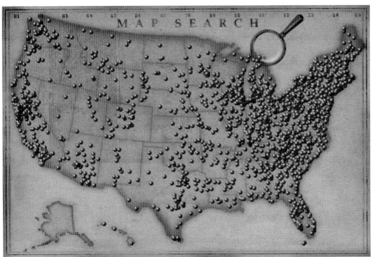

Discover books about the town where you grew up, the cities where your friends and families live, the town where your parents met, or even that retirement spot you've been dreaming about. Our Web site provides history lovers with exclusive deals, advanced notification about new titles, e-mail alerts of author events, and much more.

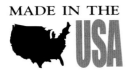

MADE IN THE USA

Arcadia Publishing, the leading local history publisher in the United States, is committed to making history accessible and meaningful through publishing books that celebrate and preserve the heritage of America's people and places. Consistent with our mission to preserve history on a local level, this book was printed in South Carolina on American-made paper and manufactured entirely in the United States.

This book carries the accredited Forest Stewardship Council (FSC) label and is printed on 100 percent FSC-certified paper. Products carrying the FSC label are independently certified to assure consumers that they come from forests that are managed to meet the social, economic, and ecological needs of present and future generations.

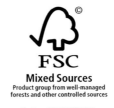

FSC
Mixed Sources
Product group from well-managed
forests and other controlled sources

Cert no. SW-COC-001530
www.fsc.org
© 1996 Forest Stewardship Council

Find Your Place in History.